LOVE, HATE AND SEX

S.N. BOSE

BOOKS FOR ALL
[A Division of D.K. Publishers Distributors (P) Ltd.]
Delhi-110 052

Sales Office :
D.K. Publishers Distributors (P) Ltd.
1, Ansari Road, Darya Ganj,
New Delhi-110 002
Phone : 3261465, 3278368
Fax : 091-011-3264368

S.N. BOSE (b. 1921-)
ISBN 81-7386-118-8

Published by :
Books For All
[A Division of D.K. Publishers Distributors (P) Ltd.]
Regd. Office : A-6, Nimri Community Centre,
Near Ashok Vihar, Phase IV, Delhi-110 052.
Phone : 7120113

Laser Typeset by :
Classic Computer Services, Delhi-110 041

Printed at :
D.K. Fine Art Press (P) Ltd.,
Delhi-110 052,

PRINTED IN INDIA

To

My Wife

Suchita Bose

ACKNOWLEDGEMENTS

Dr. Anil Gupta, a Cardiologist and a friend of mine is my inspiration to write this book. He has been guiding and encouraging me all through to write this book.

Mr. D.P. Ghose, Retired Senior Executive of Brooke Bond India Ltd. and Mr. P.K. Mitra, Retired Senior Electrical Engineer of Andrew Yule and Company, helped me in collecting a lot of information and document for this book.

I shall remain ever grateful to all these persons.

S.N. BOSE

FOREWORD

The author has made an attempt to bring out a book on the lines of a scripture. The language is lucid and will be easily assimilated by the lay person.

The book contains information, which in our busy life, we gloss over and fall in the clutches of Thanatos, as the author says.

He has transcribed life from the time of conception till the final stages.

The author, with his long experience in life, along with the citation of works of salient persons, has been able to bring out the benefits of Meditation and Yoga for our emancipation.

15th Nov. '93
New Delhi

Dr. Anil Gupta

PREFACE

The common man does not care to know as to how he was born and how he is to rear his child to enable him to safeguard himself from the inevitable pitfalls during his life span. He does not know either, what is the share of responsibility for the rearing mother. To know all these, an attempt has been made in this book to expose Miracle of Birth and reveal the inter-relation of *Love*, *Hate* and *Sex*. The interaction of *Id*, Ego and Super Ego in this regard are also dealt with.

Guidelines have been drawn from the experiences of great men, and the consequent results of the experiments by great philosophers and psychologists are also cited.

It has been written, in a lucid style to explain how right proportions of libido and mortido can transform us miraculously. The miracles of sex and the intricacies of conception, are told with illustrations, which every adult has the right to know.

It is highlighted in the book that mother's role is so very important from the conception, till the child is three years old, for all its mental developments.

The controversy of environment and the heredity is exposed in regard to the developments of a child. The present day controversy of the uplifting and the supremacy of women has been contested and thumped on.

Lastly, it is explicitly told how emancipation is possible by Meditation and Yoga and that miracles are achieved by prayers also.

S.N. BOSE

CONTENTS

1
THE THREE BASIC ELEMENTS IN US

From all the possible scientific investigations we have known, that we human beings are the best living creatures on earth. As to how we were born and how we are transformed in to this state and how long it took to culminate to this state is rather a long story.

We agree that once we get pleasure, we consider that all our basic needs are fulfilled. This pleasure may be achieved by meeting all our wants, sexual or otherwise. This ultimate goal of pleasure can be harnessed if we are happy. Animals are happy if only two basic needs are fulfilled. If they are healthy and have got enough to eat, they are happy. But, we human beings, are seldom happy, inspite of better amenities of life and better intelligence to understand and enjoy the happiness than the animals. This gift of God has got an ambiguous function. Our capacity to think, play a double role in our life. On one hand, we enjoy our amenities and the environment if it suits our choice and need. But when these do not comply with our need or temperament or choice we hate it. We develop an aversion for the situation, the elements or the persons responsible for it.

All these good and bad emotions that we come across are recorded in our brain and are retained in the furrows of the brain. The deeper impressions are retained for a longer time and are ready to be recalled later. An American psychologist, Professor Edward L. Throndike (1874-1949) worked in Harvard and Columbia for a long time and in 1914 he wrote a book, "The Psychology of Learning". From his works we get to know about "Learning, Retention, and Recall etc." Professor Throndike is recognised as the foremost authority on the studies of learning. As Dr. Abraham Sperling points out, human learning is more of planned and purposeful learning than the mechanical and uncomprehending animal learning, and that man learns more rapidly than the animals because animals cannot employ reasoning. 'Recall' is a term used by the psychologists as we use the term Replay, for playing pre-recorded taped messages.

Better the message retained in the brain, better are the chances of recall.

But psychologists have not yet been able to discover the nature of the physical changes that presumably embody retaining. We can thus, only study the 'Retention' by measuring the rate at which it declines.

What do we forget? There are two theories of forgetting:-

(a) Atrophy theory, based on metabolism;

(b) Interference theory, based on behaviourism.

Atrophy Theory

In this, forgetting results from a progressive decay of memory traces and nervous system, particularly that is found in certain diseases and in senile condition at a very advanced age.

Interference Theory

However, we are more concerned here, with most of the everyday forgetting probably caused by:

(a) Interference and

(b) Confusion, of the old with the new, rather than by a gradual fading away of old memory traces.

All these short discussions regarding learning, recall etc. were necessary for you, to understand as to why and how all those we learn on the mother's lap are not retained or even if retained, not recalled?

We have known earlier, that we human beings want happiness above all. To become happy, all of us try to meet our basic needs from our very infancy. In the infancy, personal comfort and hunger are the two prime factors. Both these needs are met adequately by the mother and the child feels happy. These showerings of love by the mother are all recorded or 'learned' in the brain and remains there till these are distorted by:

(a) Interference or

(b) Confusion (old and new recordings)

The distorting factors are many. Those may be interferences from the friends and the society which are not in tune with the learnings already recorded in the brain or due to new and different ways of living as against the old learning from the parents of the child. The result is, agony and woe in the growing child. Both the periods before and after reaching the adolescent stage of a child is very precarious.

During this transition period, when the child gets lesser and lesser attachments and care from the parents and starts developing more and more contacts with the outside world, his shield of Super Ego get thinner and thinner and gradually he develops his own ego. His personality is developed as according to the quality and quantity of his ego, that he will have developed in him.

As he grows, his 'Love Shield' from his parents gets weakened and is further supplemented by the 'Love Shield' from the school, society and other environments. During this process he has attained his adolescence.

By this time he has learnt that life is not all love. When he is confronted with bare facts of life, he perceives that it is not possible to love all. He becomes selective by now, and he develops hatred to the situations or persons he cannot match with. At the mid point of his adolescence period, he has a peculiar perception for an image for sex or rather he perceives some symbols of sex.

Though according to Sigmund Freud, the awareness of sex starts from the very infancy, some psychologists opine that the awareness of sex starts even before the child is born.

As a matter of fact, we human beings are born with all the three basic elements:

(a) Love

(b) Hate and

(c) Sex.

We have to see, how these three inherited basic elements can be tuned profitably to achieve Perfect Happiness, our Ultimate Goal! But the average man is seldom happy. That is why:

William Blake (1757-1827) wrote:—

"A mark in every face I meet,
Marks of weakness, marks of woe".

This was written about 200 years back. People were unhappy even then. But why? Why cannot we smile or have a hearty laugh atleast occasionally? We are all running up for hunting of pleasure. We are all the time in that merry go round, but pleasure remains a myth or a mirage only.

We want food to eat, clothes to cover up and house to live in. After these basic needs are met, we crave for something more. We human beings are social animals and hence our natural tendency to live in a society, as the animals love to live in herds. We want to exchange thoughts, we want to 'Love' and 'Be Loved'. Like animals, we have an urge for sexual satisfaction too.

The two elements, Love and Sex are so closely related that the picture of one is not complete without the other. Sex without Love is criminal. I did not use the word brutal, because even animals do have love play prior to the act of sex. That is the rule of the game. Comparing the act of sex for the animals with that of the homosapiens, we know that animals have particular seasons for having sex, but human beings are, these days, prone to have sex at the earliest opportunity. In a way, animals are more disciplined in the act of sex.

Why this anomaly in our society and what is the remedy thereof?

To solve this problem we have to understand a schematic diagram shown in Fig. 1.

Much of this element of Love is hereditary. From the birth, mother's love becomes a positive asset to the child till the age of 3, till the father takes over partially and continues till the child is 10 years of age. From the Fig. 1, it will be revealed that the 'Love Shield' prepared by the parents, is further fortified by the School and the Church, as the child steps into adolescence from his childhood. When the person treads the threshold of adulthood, his previous recordings of the childhood from the parents are reinforced by the contributions from the school and the Church. The recordings of the adolescence are 'Replayed' or 'Recalled', during the adult-hood. If these recordings, are profound and exciting, these will help the young to prevent him from drifting away from the just path. If these "Recordings" of the childhood and the adolescence are strong enough then, any

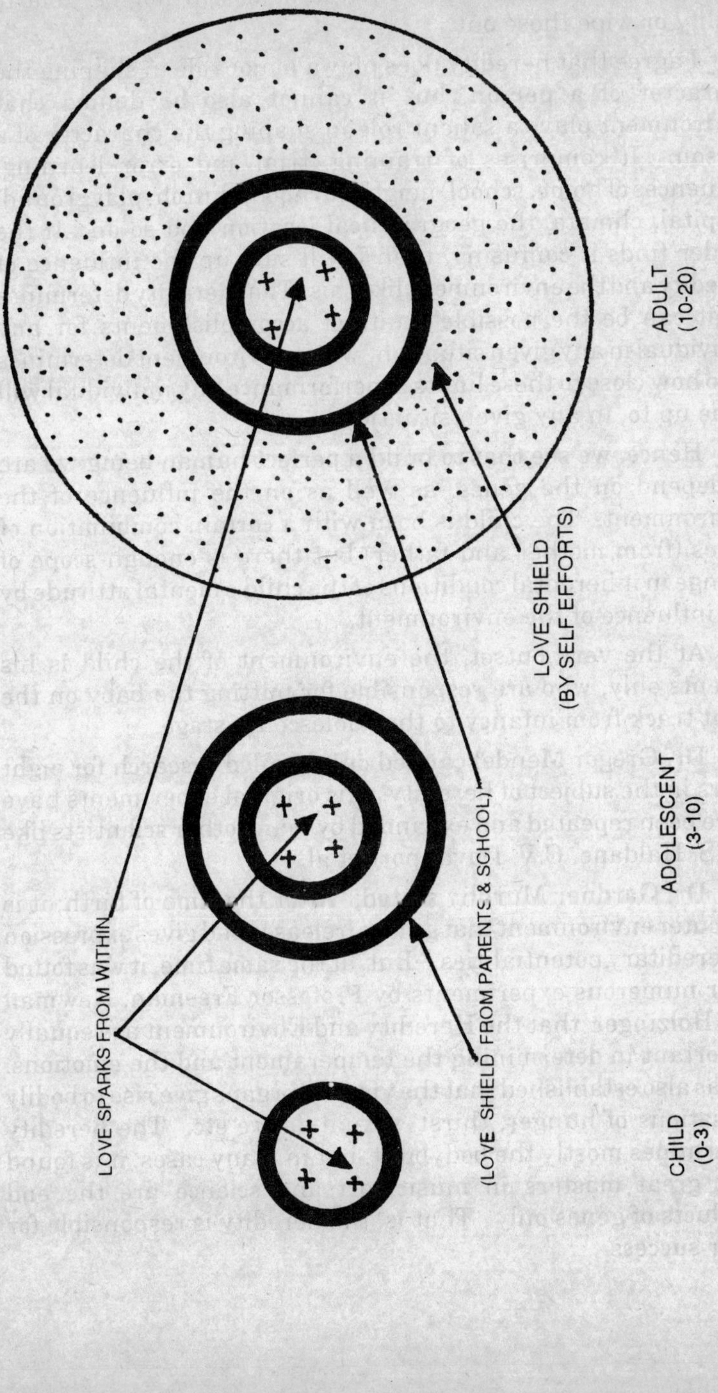
LOVE SPARKS FROM WITHIN
(LOVE SHIELD FROM PARENTS & SCHOOL)
LOVE SHIELD
(BY SELF EFFORTS)
CHILD
(0-3)
ADOLESCENT
(3-10)
ADULT
(10-20)

Fig. 1

negative emotion from the environment will not be able to nullify or wipe those out.

I agree that heredity does play a major role in shaping the character of a person, but it cannot also be denied that environment plays a salient role in shaping the character of a person. It comprises of training, trial and error learning, influences ofhome, school, neighbourhood, church, playground, hospital, climate, the geographical location and so on. If the reader finds it confusing, then I will sum up the influence of heredity and the environment like this. That heredity determines what can be the possible limits of accomplishments for any individual in any given situation, while environment determines as to how close to these limits of performance any individual will come up to, in any given situation.

Hence, we see that to build a perfect human being we are to depend on the genes, as well as on the influence of the environment. The child is born with a certain combination of genes (from mother and father) but there is enough scope of change in inherental conditions of the child's mental attitude by the influence of the environment.

At the very outset, the environment of the child is his parents only, who are responsible for putting the baby on the right track from infancy to the adolescence stage.

Dr. Gregor Mendel carried out detailed research for eight years in the subject of heredity. His original experiments have since been repeated and expanded by many other scientists like J.B.S. Haldane, C.V. Davanport et al.

Dr. Gardner Murphy stated, "After the time of birth; it is the outer environment that guides, releases and gives expression to hereditary potentialities." But, at the same time, it was found after numerous experiments by Professor Freeman, Newman and Holzinger, that the Heredity and Environment are equally important in determining the temperament and the emotions. It was also established that the visceral organs give rise to bodily sensations of hunger, thirst, sexual desire etc. The heredity determines mostly the bodybuilt, but in many cases, it is found that great masters in music, art and science are the end products of genes only. That is, the heredity is responsible for their success.

Though it is difficult to change the physical traits by environmental efforts, the environment on the other hand can groom us to the desired goal of temperament.

As I have already told earlier, the period at the threshold to the adult-hood is very important for any man or woman, but the die is cast then only. Later it depends on how much these recordings are utilised by the young person.

Father of Sri Ashutosh Mukherjee, the "Royal Bengal Tiger," as he used to be called then, had shaped the character of his son, only when he was young, by creating an interest in the boy for purchasing and reading books. Later, he not only got Knighthood from the British Empire, but became a great literary person of his time and also was the Judge of the Calcutta High Court.

You may get sufficient, good hints to rear a youngman in my book, "How to be Happy, Healthy and Rich." In that you will find the detailed methods of rearing a child from the infancy into the adult-hood, thereby making a normal and a balanced citizen with controlled 'Emotions', which will guide him to safeguard from the clutches of Emotionally Induced Illness (E.I.I.).

Referring back to Fig. No. 1 above, for development of the child from adolescence into adult-hood, you will find that at the 'Child Stage', the infant gets 'Love Sparks' from his parents. Upto the age of three, we call the period as 'Infancy'. During this period, most of the 'Love Sparks' are installed in the Infant Child. Truly speaking, 'Childhood' refers to the entire period between conception and maturity. Generally a child gets maturity when he crosses the teen age, that is when he is just 20 years old. By this time, he would have covered nearly a third of his normal life expectancy.

As to how the mother's egg is fertilised by the father's spermatoza and what happens latter upto the birth of the child will be discussed at a later stage of the book in the chapter on Sex. However, we will see how the physical and mental developments occur at various stages till the body reaches the age of 20.

Though psychologically life beings at the physical birth only, but we have reasons to believe that the pregnant woman can somehow, mark her baby by her thought, experiences and emotions. Some go to this length to say that if the period of pregnancy is a happy one for the mother, the child will have a cheerful temperament. However, research work is being carried to establish these facts.

As the child grows into adolescence (from the age of 3 onwards), he is richer with more of 'Love Sparks' from his mother. At this juncture, apart from mother's love, father also starts contributing to the bestowing of love to the child. Previously children used to start going to school from the age of five or six. But now-a-days they are sent to the school at the age of three or even much earlier. Hence at this time, he gets exposure from the outside world also.

It will be seen from the Fig. 1 that as the child moves from the first stage to the second stage (in the adolescent period), his already acquired 'Love Sparks' get developed and over and above, the love from his father and the school, fortifies the 'Love Shield', which protects the child from the adverse effects of the environment.

Games Child Play

In the adolescent period he indulges in plays and games. Generally, the parents give less importance to the games the child plays. But games play an important role in the child's development in several ways:

(a) Physically, (b) Socially and (c) Educationally.

Physically, games help to develop the child to grow muscles and enhances his motor activities. His tense and irritable character is also eased out by playing games. Socially, games develop his attitude and the adjustments regarding behaviour. He tends to be more cooperative with other members of the society. Educationally, games help to develop his sense of perception in many spheres like, shape, size, weight, colour, sound, time, distance et al.

All these are the positive aspects that the child gains during this period. But, along with these it is likely that he may develop some other elements also like Hate and Sex which were originally inherent in him. It is likely that the environment may either boost or suppress these inherent basic elements.

Great efforts will be necessary on the part of the youth, to prevent devastation of the beautiful citadel, built upto the adolescence stage by a few jolts of the environmental shocks.

Good and Bad People

Have you ever thought why some men are sages and some hooligans, what make them so?

According to Dr. Abraham Sperling and Dr. H.S. Gill of America, heredity does not count in developing a child to a particular pattern. It only lays down the essential foundations for human development. But the environment in turn is also able to alter these foundations; it may be for the better or for worse.

If you again refer to the Fig. 1 you will see that during the period from the age of 10 to 20, the adult mind which was already charged with 'Love Sparks' from the parent and the school (environment), two more things happen to him.

(a) Positive Emotions (Love Sparks) 'Generated by Self efforts' form a 'Love Shield' against devastations.

(b) Negative Emotions generated by the influence of the Environment like Hate and Sex to sway him away from his steady path.

The elements of Hate and Sex are said to be the factors which influence a person rather more easily than the element of Love. The element of Love influences the mind as soothingly as is done by the moon shine. But the elements of Hate and Sex are to strong like the rays of the Sun, that these do not spare the person and cajoles to sway him to the path they desire.

In the two chapters hence, more details regarding the influence of Hate and Sex on us, will be discussed. But here, we will discuss the basic characters of Hate and Sex and their influence on us.

Ego, Super Ego and ID

To understand these, we are to learn some definitions which will frequently be used in explaining the propagation and developments of the various branches of Hate and Sex.

(*a*) *Ego*

Every one of us know what 'Ego' is. It is the individual's conception of himself. By this Ego only we learn to distinguish between self and the Environment. In reality, Ego undulates between *Super Ego* and *ID* as will be revealed from Fig. 2.

(*b*) *Super Ego*

Super Ego will be understood by the common man as an equivalent to conscience. To be more explicit, super ego is said to be that part of psyche or personality that develops from the incorporation of moral standards and prohibitions from the parents particularly the father.

(*c*) *ID*

The infant is generally in a trance of the super ego due to the influence of his parents. When he crosses over to the Second Stage (See Fig. 2) of adolescence, he sheds much of his Super Ego and starts developing his Ego. As is told above, his Ego developed by the child helps him to realise his existence with regard to the world outside.

But as he treads the threshold of adult-hood, the original primative *ID* in him takes over once again. This *ID* is actually that division of mind or psyche that is the seat of Libido, the pleasure seeking element. After puberty, the *ID* accentuates the Libido already present in the personality to satisfy mostly by body contact.

According to Sigmund Freud, this Libido is not a new aspect, developed, as if, in the adult-child. This Libido is inherent in the psyche of all personality from the very infancy. As a matter of fact, it becomes more profound only, at the advent of adult-hood.

Referring to the Fig. 2, we find that at the advent of adult-hood there is a tough fight of *ID* with Ego, wherein, the *ID* in him, tries to have his gratifications by body pleasure, the Shield of Ego that was developed during his adolescence, throttles his impulses, full liberty to make him lewd.

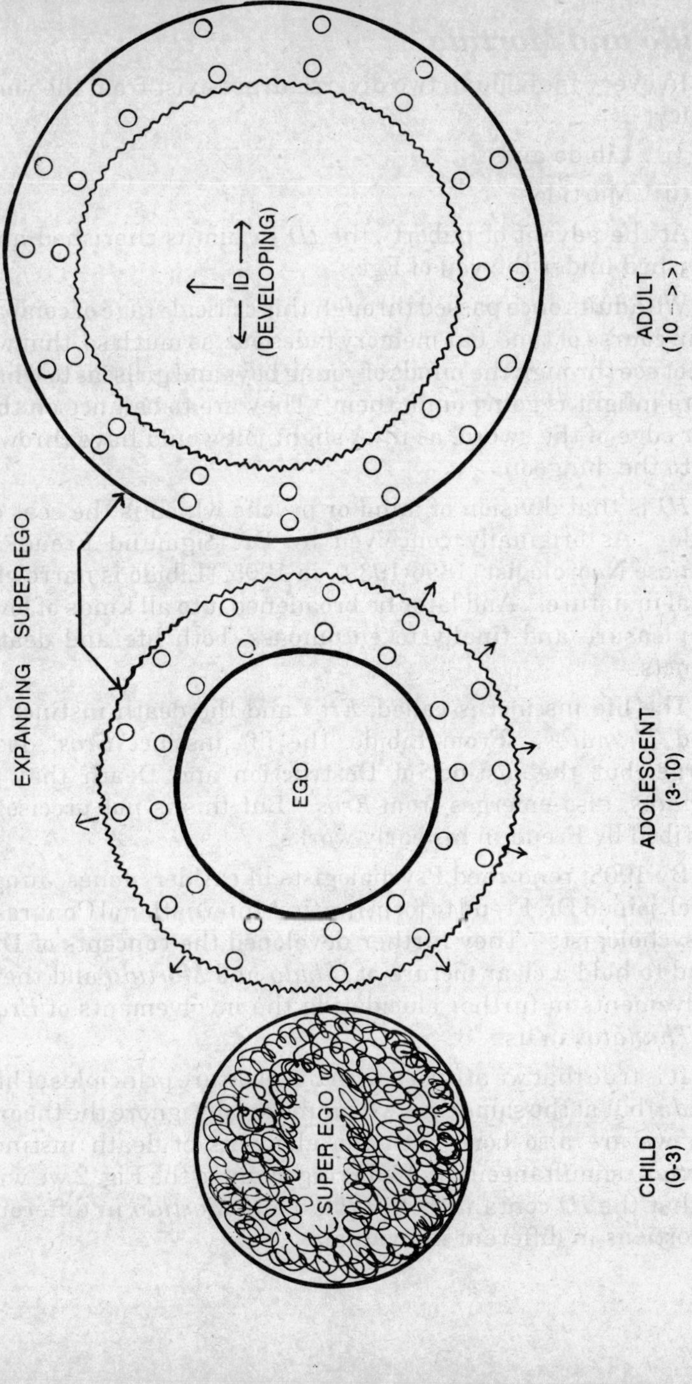
EXPANDING SUPER EGO
SUPER EGO
CHILD
(0-3)
EGO
ADOLESCENT
(3-10)
ID
(DEVELOPING)
ADULT
(10 --> >)

Fig. 2

Libido and Mortido

In every individual, two diverse urges exist from the very infancy:

(i) Libido and

(ii) Mortido.

At the advent of puberty the *ID* in him is cherished and nourished under the veil of Ego.

We adults once passed through this critical stage of combat and in course of time, our memory fades out, so much so, that we cannot see through the minds of young boys and girls, as to what severe infight is going on in them. They are to balance on the razor edge of the sword, as if. A slight jolt would have thrown him to the dungeon.

ID is that division of mind or psyche which is the seat of Libido. As originally conceived by Dr. Sigmund Freud, a Viennese Neorologist (1856-1939), in 1905, "Libido is narrowly sexual in nature." And later he broadened it to all kinds of love and pleasure and finally to encompass, both life and death instincts.

The life instinct is called, *Eros* and the death instinct is called *Thanatos*. From Libido, the life instinct *Eros*, does emerge, but the instinct of Destruction and Death that is *Thanatos*, also emerges from *Eros*. But this is not precisely described by Freud in his early works.

By 1908, renowned Psychologists like Alder, Jones, Jung, Stekel, joined Dr. Freud to form the first International Congress of Psychologists. They further developed the concepts of Dr. Freud to hold a clear picture of *Libido* and *Mortido* and their involvements in further elucidating the involvements of *Eros* and *Thanatos* in us.

It is true that we are born with the pleasure principles of life (*Libido*) but at the same time we cannot totally ignore the theory that, we are also born with the elements of death instinct (*Mortido*) simultaneously. Referring again to the Fig. 2 we will see that the *ID* contains both *Libido* and *Mortido* in different proportions in different individuals.

As to how the person nurtures the *Libido* and *Mortido* in him, depends much upon the quality and quantity of the *ID*, a particular person possesses as according to this only, a person's behavioural pattern is shaped into.

It is to be noted that the function of the *ID* of a particular person depends much on the quality and quantity of *Ego* that a person has developed and as to how he is able to control and direct his *ID* accordingly so that he becomes a *Libido Oriented* or a *Mortido Oriented* personality.

Once again, this aspect depends on three factors. Firstly, as to what his assets were when he was born (the hereditary trait), secondly as to how he was groomed by his parents at the infancy, and thirdly, on how his other environments have influenced him. Thus, the end product is a personality which may or may not steer his *Libido* and *Mortido* rightfully.

The Love Hate Tangle

Till now, we have seen that the element of the love in us, can help us considerably. This love is a natural element in us sponsored by the *Libido* present in us.

Let us now see as to how we are drifted towards Hate, as we have seen earlier, into us partially. At times it reaches beyond our control and thus we are unable to put an absolute check from hate percolating into us. Nevertheless, to sieve out much of it is possible by our own endeavour.

At birth, we mostly have unbiased ethical emotions and concepts. Since our birth, we are very close to our parents, physically and mentally, which imbibes 'Natural Love' and affection in us. This we feel all the time when we are young (in our infancy).

To follow how the element Hate in us, spreads wings and overshadows our other good qualities, we are to widen our horizon of knowledge a little further.

As we enter adult-hood, we are bombarded, as if, with various new experiences like, wants, achievements, jealousy, hate, love, frustration etc. Among all others, sex becomes more profound at this stage. Though, as according to Dr. Freud, sex is present in the newly born baby also, but at adult-hood it becomes more profound. And due to the element of sex, the interaction and the strategy, of love-hate is more evident.

Due to the natural instinct in us, we, in our infancy develop a desire to know in details about the things around us. Having an unbiased knowledge of our environment, we develop, Love for those that we come across and make an attempt to possess them and ultimately win them over.

This attitude is not only prevalent in our infancy, but it becomes a life long companion. But to possess all those, according to our desire, is not feasible. At this stage, we nurture and develop the element of Hate. This hate is a development form frustration, dissatisfaction and jealousy. However, this element of Hate will be discussed in detail later in this book.

The period from the age of 10 to 20 may be called the prime adult-hood. Then comes the period from the age of 20 to 30, when we develop those ideas and experiences gathered prior to the age of 20. If you have a close look into the people of this age group of 20 to 30, you will find that, here, in this period, people have lot of infight in Love-Hate turmoil.

Psychologists and sociologist opined that the age of 18 to 28 is precarious. During this period, great men and notorious as well as rascals, have evolved. It is a question how much Love Element have been nurtured to build the great men, or on the other hand, how much Hate element have been pumped into the other set of personalities so that these persons are having destruction and despise as their motto. During the period from 18 to 28 of age, men have made miraculous discoveries and attempted to change the world into a better place to live in.

From the judicial records also, we find that during the period from the Age of 18 to 28, most of the crimes have been hatched. The persons who could plan and hatch the crimes, some times commit the heinous crimes also.

Why is it so? Because during the adult-hood period upto the age of 18-28 years, the persons get enough liberty and opportunity to develop their basic training in various fields. Having completed that period, there comes the time to implement those that they had learnt so far.

If their parents, school, religion and friends have imbibed in them more of the element *Libido*, they will be creators of a new world. But, if on the other hand, they were encouraged and opportuned to inculcate more of *Mortido* in them, then they would turn out as destructors of the world order only.

The *Libido* as was told earlier, exists in us for developing *Eros* in us which turns us to creative attitudes. On the other hand the *Mortido* in us helps us to develop *Thanatos* which turns us to the destructive attitude.

Referring back to Fig. 2, you will find that at the third stage of adult-hood (from 20 years of age) and after (upto 30 years of age) a person gets enough opportunity to dwell upon his *ID*. This *ID*, basically has both *Libido* and *Mortido* in different proportions. This *ID* is hatched under the shield of *Ego*. If more of the *Libidanal* elements are hatched, then the person will have more of *Eros*, in him and on the other hand if *Mortidinal* elements are hatched, then the person will have more of *Thanatos* in him. This will be more explicit from the Fig. 3.

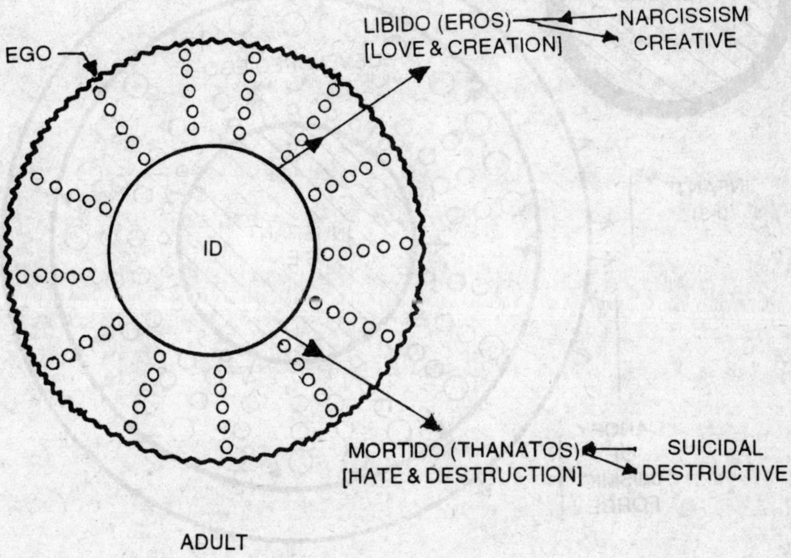

Fig. 3

It will be revealed from Fig. 3 that at the two ends of the *ID*, *Love* and *Hate* is shown. But there is no mention of *Sex* in the sketch. The reason is that whether it is *Love* or *Hate* that is prevalent in a person, he cannot have escaped from *Sex*. *Sex* undulates between *Love* and *Hate*. All these about *Sex* will be discussed in detail, in a separate chapter in this book.

At the age of 30, both men and women are generally fully mature. It is his choice, now, whether he is happy with what he possesses or he desires to become more sublime. By the time he reaches the age of 30, he or she starts realising that whatever he possesses is not all. He can increase or enrich his assets further. He starts realising the Metaphysics of Life. If a person feels the advent of this philosophy in him, he can be sucked into the cosmic canopy. This is revealed in the Fig. 4.

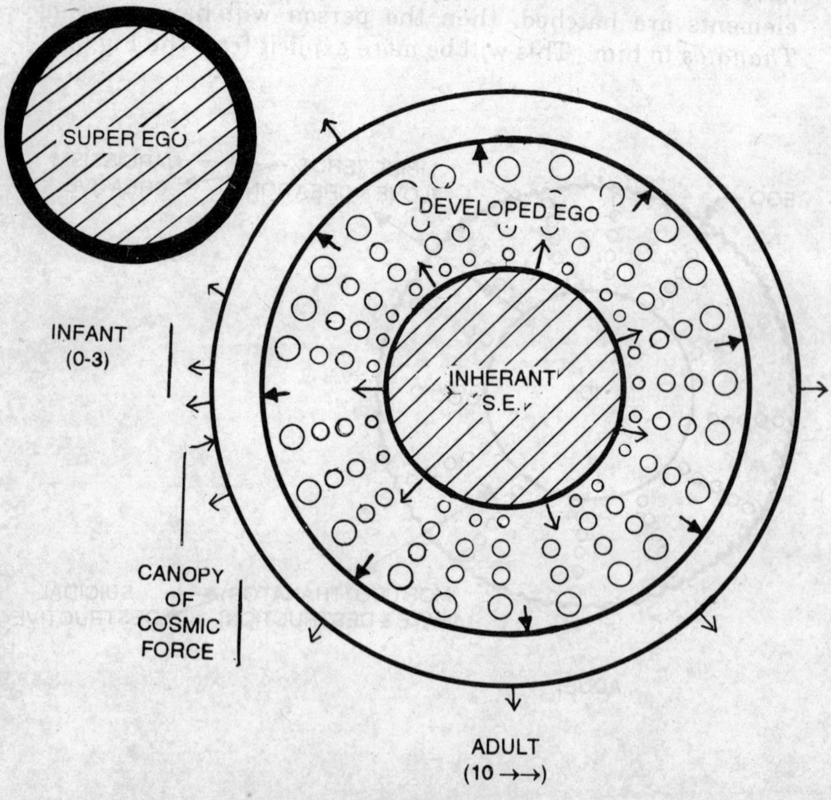

Fig. 4

As and when his *ID* is sucked in the cosmic canopy, it takes to a different form, rather a purified form. Before and after the period of 30, a battle that was going on between *Love* and *Hate* assumes the shape of war. Who wins, he rules. For women, this crucial period comes twice in them; once between 25 and 30 and again when they are in the age group from 35 and 50. If per chance, the vicious element of *Hate* wins over then the whole picture emerges differently.

These periods mentioned above for men and women, are crucial for them and they should inculcate *Meditation* and try to *Diffuse* their mind to the Cosmic Force. If you understand Metaphysics then you will realise that we can elevate the Psyche by diffusing our mind to the Great Cosmic Force.

Let us now analyse as to why and how we reach this stage. When we were but infants only, we used to feel small and insecure. But as we grow, the feeling of security grows faster than the rate of our physical growth. In the teenage stage, the feeling of, "I am the monarch of what I survey", grows very fast in us. At this stage these young boys and girls are to be injected with the idea, that "Compared to our Creator, we are merely small creatures, in this vast universe."

For this purpose, the young boys and girls should be put into special part-time vocational institutions along with their usual studies, to develop in them, the feeling of "Love, Give and Live."

This exercise, given above is for guiding the young persons, so that they do not fall a victim of *Thanatos*, the prime factor responsible for the development of *Hate* in them.

From Fig. 4, it will be evident how we can expand our domain, if we "inculcate in the practice of diffusing our mind to the 'Cosmic Force'." The young boys and girls, will then reject these negative ideas. But this is to be imbibed in them, gradually by exciting them to join the Yoga Classes for Meditation.

They should not mis-understand the idea and interpret it as an attempt to deprive them from enjoying their material and social life. They are not to stop working for procuring food, shelter and security. All other schedules will remain the same, except that whatever work they do, they are to develop 'Faith', that we are not alone in the jungle, but that the King of the Jungle is always there, to protect us and guide us if we do not loose Faith in Him.

2
LOVE

The parents we are born of, have got some 'belief' and they follow some 'doctrine' also. Unless or till we change our 'belief', our regular work schedule is guided by that doctrine only. This line of thought or belief is framed by some 'religion'. Excepting a handful of persons who do not believe in any religion, we are classed as a Hindu, Muslim, Christian, Buddhist or a Jaini.

If you read or culture any of the religions, you will find that the broad base is 'belief' and '*Love*' only. In the language of Yoga, *Love* is called Buddhaaridaya that is the heart of Buddha, the Enlightened one, a compassion for all living things, the Yoga ideal. This *Love* is a compassion for all living things. All living things mean that all things that has life. We all know that human beings and animals as well as the plants are all living things. But scientists have proved that even the things, we call inanimate, have got life. Many of us would know that even the radio-active elements have got a span of life. So, *Love* embraces all that exist on earth and in the universe.

Mother's Love - Good and Bad

In general, there are two types of *Love*, the 'acquaintance *Love*, and 'lingering *Love*'. At the first stage of life, when the baby is born, it starts loving everything that comes in its purview. Its love objects begin with mother and food. Of course, the *Hate* element is also seen in the child when it confronts with uncomfortable situations. Along the *Love-Hate Tangle*, the *Sex* urge peeps in the baby from the very infancy when it starts sucking the mother's breast or its own Thumb or Toe.

This type of *Love* that the baby gets from its mother may be called the 'acquaintance *Love*'. Earlier, in this book it is said, that mother's love is very essential and beneficial to the child. But at times, it is seen that if mother's love lacks some particular quality, that may ruin the life of the child also. Those who face life with a feeling of security are much happier than those who face it with a feeling of insecurity. At this stage of infancy, it is the affection received and not the affection given, that causes the sense of security. This sense of security comes not only from the mother's affection, but also from her admiration too. This holds good in later stages of life also. The child from whom the 'parental affection' and 'admiration' is withdrawn, is likely to become timid and unadventurous, filled with fears and self pity. He becomes an 'introvert'. He may as well become a victim of 'agoraphobia' *i.e.,* dread of open spaces. But again, the affection given must be robust and not timid. A timid mother perpetually warns her children against apprehending disasters. Yet another type of mother's affection may ruin the child. A possessive mother converts the child to a dependant person.

The off-springs of a timid mother become timid and unadventurous, filled with self-pity and unreal consolations of some system of philosophy or theology. In short he becomes an introvert.

The possessive mother rears a child, aspiring to build the child, to cope more with the world. The result is that the child becomes worse off in the long run than he would be, if he were not loved at all. When they grow, they should not be surprised if their wives regard them as grown-up children. This is all due to their unwise and possessive mother. These boys & girls become dependent all their lives.

We had digressed for sometime to highlight, as to how and how much mother's or parents' love, shapes the future of the would be grown-up man.

But separately, we are to understand the basic characters of *Love*.

In the last Chapter, we have seen, that we are born with all the three basic elements, viz., *Love*, *Hate* and *Sex*, all in different proportions mostly guided by their heredity. After birth, the infant gets mother's *Love* which supplements the inherited *Love*. Thus the element of *Love* in the child matures more and more as he continues getting mother's *Love* by body contact and strokes. The baby develops a sentiment, whose dominant characteristic is a strong feeling of affection; a *Libidinal* or *Erotic* instinct that seeks object gratification. This *Libido* as originally conceived by Sigmund Freud, is the combination of the life instinct (*Eros*) and the death instinct

(*Thanatos*). This *Libido*, as formulated by Freud, was narrowly Sexual in nature, but the concept was broadened to include all kinds of *Love* and pleasure. And it is also said that this *Love*, finally encompasses both the life and death instinct.

Though *Love*, *Hate* and *Sex* are three inseparable elements, let us first of all understand what *Love* is.

It is widely believed that *Love* is a powerful element which can enact a variety of miracles and can transcribe many things.

Technically, it is the *Libidinal* or *Erotic* instinct that seeks object gratification. But, for the common man, this *Love* is a strong feeling or attachment for a specific person, object, condition or situation and thus it's duty is feeling to achieve those. In a way, it is a type of sentiment, the dominant characteristic of which, is a strong feeling of affection or affinity. The person who is in *Love* with any other person or persons, or other entity or entities, the *Libido* or affinity for that, is directed towards seeking satisfaction which only then, culminates in completion. You will understand it better, if this factor is elucidated with concrete examples.

Suppose a young boy develops a fancy and an urge to meet a young girl of his choice. He will feel uneasy till he has met the girl. This urge for meeting the girl is *Love*, of the boy for the girl. Similarly if a kid longs to have a cake or a toy, that shows that he has got an urge to have the object, to gratify his *Libidinal* urge. His *Love* for the object or objects will achieve the level of satisfaction, only on acquiring the object. This element of *Love* is inherent in all individuals in different quantity and quality. It is rare that a person is altogether devoid of this *Libido* (the *Love* element), unless he is mentally sick.

It was told earlier also that every individual inherits some *Libido* and some *Mortido*, while in the very infancy. And during the adolescence period, he further develops these and the proportion of the said two elements are altered, as they grow, as according to their parent's influence, schooling and the influence of the other environments that he is put into.

It is seen that, in general the element *Libido* (the *Love* element) prevails on us more than *Mortido* (the *Hate* element). It is not rare either that there are persons in whom *Mortido* is prevailing more, rather than *Libido*. But this is very rare.

Think of Adolf Hitler, Alexander the Great, Changhase Khan or Saddam Hussain! Do you remember how they behaved and about their contribution to the world?

In the next chapter, we shall discuss what part this *Mortido* plays. Is this *Hate* element, all to be hated by us or has it any utility at all? According to Viennese neurologist Sigmund Freud (1856-1939), *Love* and Esteem are the prime factors that should be bestowed on the child from the very infancy, by his parents for him to grow into a mature and a square personality. Giving him good food and body contact becomes a sign of *Love* and praising his deeds becomes a sign of Esteem. *Love* and Esteem become very valuable to the child, because they result in gratification. This *Love* and Esteem promise future gratification to console him for current frustrations, as he grows.

At the infant stages, the child does not know the grammar of *Love*. He only knows that *Love* provides him with immense pleasure. As that *Sex* is embedded in *Love*, the child does not know. The child does not know much about *Love* and *Sex*, so the common man also is almost ignorant about the true concept of *Love* and *Sex*. When the child sucks the thumb or the toe, he does it for the very reason, that he derives pleasure and a sort of sexual satisfaction, as he feels as if he sucks milk from his mother's breast.

Freud told us that the activities of *Love* and *Sex*, start from the very infancy, though we are ignorant about them. But if these are steered ingenuously they can pay dividends when we are adults. That is why we should make it a point that the child should be imbibed by *Love*, and told earlier, from the very infancy, so that he can profitably store them as future assets. Mothers' cuddling, caressing and stroking from the very infancy forms the first *Love* assets for the child. As he grows, he gradually develops this for his future guidance.

If this *Love* asset is updated and harnessed well, according to the environmental circumstances, then this *Love* element in him, will not only benefit him but will benefit others as well and ultimately will engulf the whole world.

But by *Love*, the common man understands, '*Sensual Love*' only, by which he feels sensation, gratification and also orgasm. But there is yet another type of *Love*, the Puritan *Love*, and non-sensual type of *Love*. This is the type of *Love* sanctified by simplicity and, purity of worship. It is a Platonic *Love*, which is *Love* of the soul and for the soul. It is a *Love* into which, the sensual desire is supposed not to enter at all.

But thinking in line with Dr. Freud, we may argue that the *Love* is only *Erotic* and it culminates in orgasm only. But then does the Platonic *Love*, do not come in the purview of *Freudian Love*? What is Orgasm afterall? Is it not the immense sensation of pleasure which eclipses all other thoughts and action for the time being?

Have any one among you, tried to fall into Deep Meditation, for some time? If so, have you not felt the thrill, sensation and ecstasy, may be momentarily or for a short duration? If you study the life of Jesus Christ, Mohammed, Guru Nanak, Chaitanya Maha Prabhu, you will know that they were prophets of *Love*, they were embodiment of *Love*. Whoever came in close contact with them, felt the sensation of pleasure and ecstasy.

By now, we have learnt that *Love* is a very essential element for us to live. But we should know as to how, when and how much *Love* we should impart to and to whom. If that is not done the end product will not be homogeneous and effective. An analogy will help you to understand it better.

When the doctor prescribes some medicine, he indicates the following things:

(a) Which medicine should be taken for which ailment;

(b) The strength or potency of the medicine.

(c) The frequency of administration.

(d) Tho quantity of the medicine to be taken each time.

(e) The time of the day, when the medicines are to be taken.

(f) The method of taking the medicine (In 'Ayurvedic', it is called Anupan).

Similarly, *Love* should not be administered with zest and zeal without going into details of the administration. I have seen young persons being spoiled due to unmethodical *Love*. Whatever is true for *Love*, is also true for *Hate* and *Sex*. All these should be practiced with the skill of an artisan to achieve perfection. The balanced proportions of all the three elements of *Love, Hate* and *Sex* will impart perfection, maturity and pleasure.

Love can be bestowed, to all men and women, to animals and plants and to all natural elements as well as to the materials created by men. Once we groom ourselves to this behaviour of *Love* to human beings, it will not be difficult to drift and to stride over to all other entities mentioned above. Thus, we may gradually, transform all love into the universal *Love*. This *Love* has got a peculiar property. Like the third law of dynamics, your *Love* bears fruit, sooner or later. If you *Love*, you become loveable also.

Types of Love

Love can be broadly classified in three groups; viz:

(a) *Erotic Love* (*Sexy*).

(b) *Regard Love* (*Respect*).

(c) *Affectionate Love* (*Pity*).

To understand the functions graphically, we may term them as below;

(a) Erotic Love or Level Love

This love, functions almost at a level, comparable to that of the lover. A lover imparts love to another person who is almost his same age, status or temperament. This is generally among two persons of the opposite sex. But in cases of sexual aberrations, it is not uncommon that a girl loving another girl or a boy loving another boy. These sexual abnormalities are dealt with in the chapter on sex.

The general trend of *Love* is *Erotic* or sexy in nature. Most often than not, it is seen that this *Erotic Love* leads to acute ecstasy and sometime it culminates in orgasm. In this erotic love, when boys and girls or men and women come closer mentally and physically they get pleasure out of the act. When they are more intimate, they get exquisite pleasure. Generally, the close mental and physical association leads to the secretion of hormones and thereby, ultimately it culminates in orgasm.

But it is also seen that similar pleasure and ecstasy is obtained when a person reaches his pinnacle of satisfaction in creating a piece of art or architecture or achieving one object of desire.

To be explicit, one may create some piece of music like that of Mozert, or a piece of fine art like that of Ruban or Leonardo-da-Vince, or Nanda Lal Bose, or a dramatist like Sisir Kumar Bhaduri. In this process of creation, he may reach ecstasy and thereby be able to consummate and have immense of pleasure, so much so, that sometimes this pleasure is comparable to the state of orgasm that is experienced after mating. He may thus reach a point of excessive pleasure irrespective of any other inherent agony of his.

Narcissism: The *Erotic Love* as discussed above, is generally between himself and any other person at his own temperamental level which may be of any sex or age. This is a type of extrovert *Love*. But if it is turned outside in, which is called introvert *Love*, then it is termed as Narcissism or "self *Love*". In this type of love, the person undergoes a sort of neurosis, in which, the *Libido*, regress to a very early phase of his development. This means that the person behaves mentally as if he has gone back several years in his life and thus behaves likewise. A person having excessive narcissism in him, fails to develop an attachment to another person or object.

It is seen, in general, that every individual is a Narcissist to some extent. Had it not been so, he could not have been able to take care of himself and his health. On the other hand, a person who does not care for his A.D.L. (aid to daily living) and is careless in minding his own personal needs and hygiene, is said to have less Narcissism in him.

It is not rare to find, that many a person, depends mostly on some other personality like mother or wife, if they are male and brother or sister if they are female and sometimes to husband also. Sometimes they depend on his aids, like his colleagues or even subordinates.

There is a Greek mythological story spinning round Narcissism. There lived an identical twin in a forest long long ago. They were in acute love with each other. One day when they were roaming in the wilderness, one of them got drowned in a pool of water. The other was depressed and morosed and hence kept on sitting by the side of the pool of water, not taking any food or water, whatsoever. After a long time, when felt thirsty, he reached the water and found his brother's image reflected in the water. He wanted to embrace the same. It was actually his own image, and on touching the image, it got disturbed. This story went on for days together. And ultimately he got withered and died at that spot. It is said, that at that place a beautiful flower plant germinated. People around, called the flower that blossomed as Narcissous, after the name of that young boy that died. Narcissous and his brother both loved each other and one loved the image of his brother in the water and died. Hence loving one's own self is called Narcissism or self *Love*.

Homo - Sexual Love: When a child crosses the age of ten, he is no longer a child. He falls under the category of adolescence. His whole pattern of psychology undergoes a transformation. The adolescence is truly a time of 'Storm and Stress'. On one side he develops ideas to guide himself towards his own goal and on the other side, due to the physical changes that is going on in the boy or the girl, it weakens its continuous identity. This young person, at this time, falls in *Love*, generally with someone much older than himself. The boy locates a hero of his choice, a man-about-town, similarly young adult girls, 'play around' with girls much younger to herself for the fun of it. This is the beginning of Homo-Sexuality.

This fixation, on the adults that of his own sex, begins with the parents and is absolutely normal upto the age of nine. From the age of ten or eleven, the adolescent boys and girls, try to find some person or persons other than their parents for satisfying their *Love*. For a few years hence, they are deeply attached to another child of their own age and sex. This homo-sexual stage is perfectly innocent and normal between the age of 10 and 15. This is the period when the boys and girls try to free their bondage from their parents.

Till the period that the boys and girls attain puberty, they try to avoid their mate of the same sex. This is the period from the age of 10 to 15 for boys and girls, that they are homo-sexual. But this homo-sexuality is quite normal. Later, when the normal sexual development occurs, the boys and girls go in to share *Love* with a person of about the same age but of the opposite *Sex*.

But if again, if the boys and girls try to satisfy their *Love* with a person or persons of the same *Sex* before and after they reach the age of 20 then that is abnormal. This is Homo-Sexuality in the true sense.

This Homo-Sexuality is dealt with in details in the chapter on *Sex* in this book later.

(b) Regard Love (Respect) or (Elevated Love)

If we regard some body superior to us, *Love* some person of an elevated status, then this *Love* may be termed as Regard *Love*. The object of this *Love* may be animate or inanimate. We may *Love* a country, a Nation or a Religion or a person per excellence, this as well will be termed as Regard *Love* or Respect *Love*.

As 'Regard *Love*' is for an elevated status, we are to look upwards for this also. Hence, in order to enable us for this act, our attitude eventually, will be elevated. As a matter of fact, it is not only our attitude but our whole psyche gets elevated and refined.

A simple example will elucidate this. When we go to a temple or a place of worship, we do not go shabby or unclean, physically or mentally. We rather, make some preparation for the visit to the shrine. The preparation itself elevates us.

Let us, once again, go back to our infancy. We *Love* our parents unbiased. But as we grow, we approach them with bashful look and with somewhat biased mind. Why this happens? To be able to approach them, the adolescent child is to congregate enough of courage and shed much of his ego. This is nothing but some preparation for the approach. This exercise is somewhat similar to that for the preparation before visiting a place of worship, as mentioned above.

You cannot *Love* a person or a thing or a situation all of a sudden, without some preparation for it. There has to have some cause or reason for you to fall in *Love*. The child *Love*s his mother because he gets milk, comfort and caressing and cuddling.

You *Love* a scenery or a piece of art or music, because it pleases your senses and gives a soothing effect on your nerves. Similarly if you *Love* a girl, she gives a soothing sensation on you in return. You *Love* her not for nothing. But all these can be categorised as "*Love* at first sight." But these types of *Love* do not last longer unless they are positioned on a broad base, for better equilibrium. If you love a girl or love your boss at the office or your office work itself, these are postulates only and must be backed by profitable propositions.

I shall relate a story to illustrate this type of *Love* which on the face of it seems to be only a *Love* at first sight only. There lived a boy, very obedient to his father. His father observed that every evening he used to come home late. One day he stood at the gate to nab him red handed. He asked the boy, as to where he had spent all these hours in the evening. The boy answered that as he loved the girl next door, he goes there every evening. The father lost his temper. The boy answered, "Sir, you told me that our Lord Jesus told us that if we *Love* our neighbour, it is as good as loving HIM." At that the father was non-plussed. In the story, the boy obeyed his father and as he respected our Lord, he did as was desired by HIM. Here the *Love* was not for nothing.

You have seen in the last Chapter that we are born with some inherited *Love* and gradually it is further supplemented by the Mother's *Love*. As we grow, the potentiality of *Love* increases and this process goes on till death. But during the course of our life the shape of *Love* changes, sometime it is strong and at times it dwindles down so much that we almost loose track of it. This is the opportune time, to supplement with "*Love* of a stronger quality," which does not fade out easily and we are not swayed away and we do not loose our well planned track.

At the time of hormone changes in men and women, we get mentally disturbed. For men the periods are 14, 40 & 60 and for women the periods are 12, 18, 40 & 55. These are the periods when they must be guided well, so that "Mortidinal" elements present in them do not win them over, and change their traits altogether. Both for men and women, the periods when there are more chances for them to be swayed away from their planned track is 40. Round about this age of 40, all persons should be baptised to some particular sanctity or they should be coaxed to join the course of Yoga, where Meditation is taught and practiced, if they had not done so earlier. This is the supreme method to save ourselves from the impending clutches of *Mortido*. As already discussed *Libido* leads us to creative attitude and *Mortido* towards destructive attitude.

For example many a people, start taking medicines, as soon as they feel feverish. Similarly, we must inculcate in some 'Elevated *Love*' as soon as we apprehend danger of drifting towards Supreme Hate.

This 'Elevated *Love*', as was discussed earlier, in this chapter, helps us to commune with the vital force, the Great Cosmic Force. One of the methods of this commune is the practice of Transcendental Meditation (T.M.) which Maharsi Mahesh Yogi's desciples are practicing throughout the world.

(c) *Affectionate Love*

As Erotic *Love* is prevalent among people of comparable age and status and Regard *Love* is imparted to people superior to the person, the Affectionate *Love* is for the rest. This does not come under the above two groups.

This 'Affectionate *Love*' is from people of higher age and status to other people and all other animate and inanimate bodies. If you *Love* any person who is younger to you, you wish that he may be benefitted, and flourish under the guidance of the Cosmic Force. In this category not only young children, but the domestic pets, flowers and plants too, may be grouped. A piece of art or architecture also come under the same umbrella. If you *Love* your country or the men and women of a particular region then that also will come under this group.

According to Sir Issac Newton, every action has an equal and opposite reaction. Hence the *Love* that you bestow upon somebody or some thing, should have a back reaction. You get back an euphoria of *Love*, you get an asthetic satisfaction.

You will learn now, how we start loving our environment or the inanimate bodies around us!!

Dr. John Broadus Watson—an American Psychologist (1878 -1958) gave a beautiful definition of *Love*. We know that at birth, we are able to distinguish two emotional feelings; one, the discomfort involved in the stress and tension of excitement, and the other, the calm pleasure of emotion. This calm pleasure of emotion, Dr. Watson termed as *Love*. In the infancy, these general excitements can be classified as 'distress' and 'delight'. This 'distress' gives rise to Anger, Fear, Disgust, Jealousy and 'Hate'. And from 'delight' is born Love, Regard, Affection, and Pity. As we grow and reach the stage of adolescence, this *Love* of 'Delight' is transformed into the Lusty *Love* or Sexual *Love* at the advent of puberty. From the 'Distress', develops '*Hate*' from which erupts the disintegration of the world.

It is at this stage of infancy that we learn to *Love* all things that give pleasure to us whether animate or inanimate. When adult, we get enormous pleasure by expressing our likeness and *Love* to those around us and thereby get enough feed back of *Love* and pleasure.

In the infancy, we were groomed to that infantile *Love*, which was spontaneous and simple. The domain of *Love* was then very limited also; but as we grow, the *Love* initiated by the parents had taught us not only to get *Love*, but also to give *Love*. In the infancy, the *Love* received from the parents was almost instantaneous, but equivocal too. It not only taught us how to get *Love*, but gradually we were groomed, as to how we are to give *Love* to others also. At this stage, we came out from a smaller circle to a rather bigger circle. In a way, the domain of *Love* is widened. We gradually learn to *Love* things and persons other than the parents. We learn to *Love* and develop compassion for domestic pets, birds, and animals. We ultimately learn to *Love* the plants and the nature in general.

So far, so good; as we grow a little older, and cross the age of 40; the real trouble starts. The aura of parental *Love* fades out and those developed by our own ego also are shattered by the concussion of the hard core realities of life. By this time, we encounter many realities of life, like death, punishment to the deserving as well as to the undeserving, the envy, jealousy, cheating, hatred etc. This is the time when our mind gets disturbed or distorted and we are likely to be devastated. This is the time when we get drifted more and more towards the *Thanatos*; the death elements, the monarch for *Hate*.

There are two ways out to save our soul. One, to combat the effect of *Thanatos* by the inherited, and gifted *Eros* from the parents, as well as those developed by the environmental influences. Most of the time it is seen that it is the *Thanatos* that wins the game.

To nullify the effects of *Thanatos*, there is another unique way out. We should try to surrender to the Universal Vital Force and allow our Own Vital force to get emancipated. Strike a contract with 'Nature'. This will be easy to understand if we look back to Fig. 4.

If we can inculcate this attitude, then the work is done. The Aura of *Love*', is expanded and spread over all those animate and inanimate bodies. We then are equipped with more *Eros* to eclipse the effects of *Thanatos*.

Love not only can promote cohesion, but also creation, whereas *Hate* promulgates destruction, which may lead to total annihilation.

3

HATE

In the previous chapters, we have seen that we are born with three basic elements; *Love*, *Hate* and *Sex* in different proportions. As we grow, the element of *Love* stops growing fast and the elements of *Hate* and *Sex* engulfs us to a large extent. First *Hate* takes over and then the *Sex*. It depends on our previous grooming by our parents and school, how and how much we can combat either to win over or to succumb to the elements of *Hate* and *Sex*.

The 'Stubbornness' pops its head at the very age of three. The child reacts to aggressive suggestions by refusing to comply with adult requests. But this aggressive and stubborn attitude 'declines' later after the age of three. At the age of four, 'Rivalry', takes over and after four he develops 'Jealousy'. Statistics indicate that out of three jealous children, two are girls. It is also seen that children of higher intelligence are rather more jealous than the others. But this jealousy again, decreases from the age of five when the children begins to develop interests outside his limited parameter, (that is his home).

It is to be noted that I have used the words, "declines" and "decreases" only for the behaviours like stubbornness, aggressiveness, jealousy etc., because these do not stop at this point, but dwindles down a bit and lingers throughout the life span.

All these make the person worry for himself as well as for others. He becomes *Envy*, and this, at times, leads him to be 'Angry' when 'Frustrated'. *'Envy'* is such an element that the envious person develops hatred and this *Hate*, in turn, promotes 'Anger'.

If these are not checked or throttled at the very outset, that is during the teenage only, then these may, ultimately ruin the future of the person when grown up. We generally envy a person or a situation out of any emotion only, whether it is justifiable or not. It is seen that we are envious more for the persons rather than for the situations. This envy promotes jealousy. The development of jealousy after the age of four is a natural phenomenon. It is the duty of the parents to see that the jealousy does not get an opportunity, to make a headway, which otherwise may cause ample damage to the person when grown up. Envy is one of the most universal and deep-seated human passions and jealousy is a special development from this Envy. Not only the envious person wishes to inflict pain and agony to others but he himself is rendered unhappy by this Envy.

Instead of deriving pleasure from what he has, he derives pain from what others have. This passion of Envy may become fatal to the excellence and the most useful exercise of exceptional skill. But there is a way out for respite from this catastrophy. In human nature, there is a quality for compensating this passion. This is called 'Admiration'. This admiration may increase human happiness and diminish 'Envy'. If we are wise, we would not be envious for what we do not have but others have. But on the other hand, we should try to achieve those, which others have, by making ourselves more knowledgeable and efficient and by congregating more energy and skill to acquire those things. Envy is one form of vice. It is partly moral and partly intellectual which consists in seeing things never in themselves but only in others. For all these, the proper remedy is only the mental discipline, that is the habit of not thinking fruitless thoughts. If we can cure ourselves of Envy, we can acquire happiness and become enviable ourselves.

Envy & Hate

For achieving glory, we may envy Napoleon. But Napoleon envied Caesar, Caesar envied Alexander and then Alexander envied Hercules. But you know, Hercules was only an imaginary character; he never existed. Hence, we cannot get away from envy by means of success alone, as we will find that somebody or other may be in a more advantageous position than us. We can only get away from this Envy by enjoying the pleasures that come on our way while doing our own work. We should avoid complexes by comparing our situations with those that we imagine to be more fortunate than ourselves.

Envy is an evil, no doubt, but it is an evil which must be endured in order to arrive at a more justifiable social system. As a matter of fact, all bad things are inter-connected. Fatigue very frequently is the cause of *Envy*. When a person feels inadequate to propagate his work, he feels a general discontentment which is liable to generate *Envy* towards those whose works are not critisized or scrutinized by others. At this situation, one develops 'Fatigue'. But it is also seen that many a times the *Envy* which apparently seems to be purely professional in nature, really it may have a 'Sexual' source also. A man or a woman who is married happily and is rearing their children well, are seldom seen to be envious to others at work. The positive pleasure of mankind has been increased a number of times due to the modernisation of our society, but there is no doubt that we are more prone to *Envy* and hatred than our predecessors.

All these said above, are due to the effect of *Thanatos* present in us. *Thanatos*, the death instinct, the provoker of the element of *Hate* in us, manipulates all these to make us more unhappy. Now, we have known, what all cause to develop *Hate* in us. But first of all, we must know what basically, *Hate* is? Hate is a strong adverse attitude of one's own self which proves a person to dislike intensely, some person or persons, object or situation, involving anger, which leads to the desire to inflict injury on the person, object or situation and ultimately having a desire to destroy or kill the same.

It is the Law of Nature that all things in this universe have got some longevity and after the lapse of that period everything is deemed to be doomed for destruction. This is a natural death of an object. But that does not solve our problem. If we cannot meet our ends, if we cannot fulfil our desire, to reach our personal goal, then we become envious, and thereby, we become jealous. There begins the activities of the demon *Thanatos*. We thus pave the way for the demon to travel upto us and destroy us and ultimately the whole life on earth is devastated.

Is Hate So Bad?

But is the element of *Hate* that bad? Do we have to exercise our will power to destroy the demon, if it is creating so much of havoc? What is ill must be won over by our will power. If a person or group of persons, or a swarm of insects or herd of animals that are trying to disrupt the normal life on earth, then those should of course be prevented from doing so. And, in order to achieve our goal sometimes we are to *Hate* those, resist them from their activities and at times, it may become necessary to destroy them also. Even in the sacred Epic of Indian Mythology 'The Bhagwat Geeta' it is said that this act of *Hate* and violence is neither un-social nor un-ethical. War is not always violence, neither is an unethical act. Many a times, it is seen that war is fought to end a war.

You will find in Fig. 3 that the two basic characteristics of human beings is a mixture of *Libido* and *Mortido*, in different proportions in different persons at different stages of life, which makes a man or a woman behave differently.

That, *Mortido* is an essential factor in human beings is an established fact. Man is not complete if he is not a mixture of *Libido* and *Mortido*. You cannot possibly do away with *Mortido* altogether. An example will elucidate this. Everybody knows that friction is an impediment to the fast progress of the mechanical life. Every effort is made to minimise this friction by providing ball and roller bearings, by applying lubricating oil and grease also to the mating surfaces. Thereby, lubrication has been classified as a separate science.

Have you ever thought what would have happened if there was no friction at all? First of all, I and you would not be able to walk on the road without friction. You could not put a nail on the wall or drive a screw in to any wood work that you intended to build up, without the existence of friction. Similarly if people were devoid of *Mortido*, the carpenter would not be able to cut wood (as it is a destructive work), the turner would not be able to shape an article on lathe machine (as cutting an object is a destructive job also), the butcher would not be able to cut meat, for fear of similar vice. Or even your wife would not be able to chop fruits and vegetables, as cutting with a sharp weapon like knife would also be a vicious act. Hence *Mortido* will be there in us to survive but we are to see that it does not put its head up beyond limit.

Libido is the *Sex* instinct of a person which seeks Erotic pleasure. Whereas *Mortido* is the death instinct, provoking hatred. Whereas *Libido* advocates *Love* and creation, the *Mortido* has got a tendency for development of hatred and destruction. Usually, the Libidinal forces tend to promote love and affection and help us in the act of creation. But if the same is directed outside in, the result is Narcissism in which the *Libido* regresses to a very early (prenatal) phase of development. The person, fails to develop an attachment for another person or object and starts loving his or her own self. On the other hand, in the second half of the personality, if the dorment *Mortido* gets activated and is directed outwardly, then the person is activated for destruction. He will *Hate* everything other than himself. But if on the other hand, this urge for destruction is turned outside in, then, the person may try to commit suicide also; an attempt for self destruction.

Before we deal in details of what *Mortido* directs *Thanatos* to do, we may get opinions of some of the prime psychologists. Sigmund Freud wrote in 1920, in his monograph, *Beyond the Pleasure Principle*, - "that the conservative character of the instinctual life posits a psychic conflict of two primordial drives, viz.; *Eros* and *Thanatos*". *Eros*, is the term adopted by Freud from the name of the Greek God of Love, to mean all of the life or the self preservation instinct. *Eros* the life - instinct preserves the organic substance and binds it into ever larger units; - that is family, tribe, society, nation and the like.

Antithesis to *Eros* is *Thanatos*. The Greek Word *Thanatos* literally means death. This *Thanatos*, the death instinct seeks to dissolve these units and reinstate their antecedent in organic states. Part of this death instinct, becomes directed towards the outer world manifesting itself as destruction and aggression.

"This pungent death instinct *Thanatos*, is such, that any cessation of the outward flow causes this energy to be internalised, intensifying the self destruction, always continuing within and the two instincts, *Eros* and *Thanatos*, seldom appear in isolation and are always mingled in various proportions", Freud wrote.

Freud again wrote in 1929, skilfully, in his, "*Civilization and Discontents*", "The tendency to destruction is an innate, independent and instinctual disposition in man. While *Eros* binds men to each other, Libidinally and socially, into a humanity, though, what we call the evolution and culture. *Thanatos* in turn, fragments and thus opposes the programme of civilization.

The struggle between the instinct of life and the instincts of destruction is what all life essentially consists of." The death instinct *Thanatos* advocates the distortion and destruction of life. Life otherwise is a thing of *Love*, a thing of beauty and really is a joy for ever.

Life is beautiful and death is horrible. A common man, generally, is *Erotic* and hence do not take death as a routine. A birth of a child gives immense pleasure to the family and at the death of a person, people get plunged into sorrow and grief. But many believe that the death is not the end of life but death is only a transformation from one life to the other. The Hindus believe that life is in the psyche of a person and that at death of the body, the psyche 'Atmah' continues to exist, because 'Atmah' is non-perishable. After the formal death of a person, the Christians do not destroy the body, but they bury it underground in a coffin, with the belief that on the day of Resurrection the Lord will come for the judgement of the person. Similarly the Muslims also bury the dead body underground in a coffin, with the belief that the Prophet will come for the Judgement of the person one day.

Prophet Mohammed is supposed to be last of the Divine Apostles and Messengers and what all he has revealed is found in the Holy Quran. It is said that there are three stages after death; the first is BARZAKH (interval between death and resurrection). When the earthly body is buried or cast into river, his soul does not perish with him. This stage maintains till the Last Day (When the entire material world will be destroyed by the command of God). In the second stage, long after the day of Annihilation, when God will wish, all men will be raised up again, to render a full account of his doings. In this Great Reckoning, people will be sorted out and will be sent to Heaven or Hell, as according to his doings. After this, at the third and the last stage, the Lord will reward those in Heaven and punish those in Hell.

In the Holy Quran, you will find the happenings of the 'Last Day' of total annihilation of the world, the raising of the men again for their judgement and finally the execution of the 'Divine Verdict' and allotment of Heaven and Hell in the Chapter - TAKVIR, INFITAR and INSHIQAQ. In the Hindu Epic, it is advocated that death does not seal the chain of generations and Atmah is unperishable.

Inspite of having known all these, the friends and relatives of the dead do lament for the diseased. But Freud's interpretations for the *Thanatologist*, the theory of "Denial of Death" is channelised and distorted to induce the belief that when at the death, the life is not finished, then why worry for the dead! Hence killing, distortion and destruction are the only means to an end. You do it because you think that you achieve something in doing it. The *Mortidines* get immense pleasure in the process of destruction. Have you not seen young boys and girls giggling after cutting the limbs of an ant or clipping the wings of a bird! And all such deeds, come under the umbrella of *Thanatos*.

This 'Denial of Death' is prevalent in most of the prominent religions of the world. It is believed that the Lord assures us that He is always present within us and it is also believed that the reincarnation and "Transformation of the Soul is a common feature."

This belief of 'Denial of Death' urges people to attach least importance to death. Death looses its reality and this no longer is thought to be a serious affair. This leads people to get involved in all sorts of anti-life activities, without qualms. Hence, in the developed countries the anti-life activities like suicide, murder abortion, rape, violence and other abnormal perversions are on the increase.

Let us now see the locus standi of *Thanatos* in our character. How this *Thanatos* fits into us and fights with *Eros*? *Thanatos* is the Greek name for the mythical personification of death, borrowed by Sigmund Freud to represent the death instinct present in all of us. The death instinct *Thanatos* is for destruction and death, chaos and calamities. When this instinct of death, *Thanatos*, is fused with the pleasure instinct *Eros*, which may be directed inwards or outwards in us, it starts activating in destroying us (if it is directed inwards, -it is suicide) or destroying others (if it is directed outwards -it is killing and destruction), for mere, 'Pleasure' only. This word 'Pleasure' is to be noted here. This enthusiasm for these acts come from the life instinct *Eros*, which originates from *Libido*, the main source of energy present in all of us. It is to be noted here that even the death instinct *Thanatos*, gets its energy from *Eros*, the pleasure principle.

It, then, be surmised that whether it is the life instinct '*Eros*' or the death Instinct *Thanatos* that is prevalent in us, we are, to get hold by the forelock, the 'Libidinal' forces that off shoots from '*Eros*' to control the activities of either or both of *Eros* and *Thanatos*. *Eros* is the symbol of life and *Love*. If you probe deeper, as was told by Freud, this *Eros* is the spring of *Love* and *Sex*. You cannot segregate *Sex* from *Love*. *Sex* is an integral part of *Love*. However the ambiguity will be deciphered in the next Chapter of *Sex* in more details.

But our problem now is that if the effect of *Mortido* is all bad, why not try to eliminate the influence or minimise it to the bare minimum. Barring a few, it is neither advisable nor possible to eliminate absolutely, the influence of *Mortido* on us. The utility of *Mortido* in us is all related a while ago, as to why and how the *Mortido* cannot be eradicated absolutely.

Anger

Take the case of Anger. It is an acute emotional reaction, elicited by any one or more number of stimulating situations, like threat, overt aggression, restraint, verbal attack, disappointment or frustration, characterised by strong responses in the Autonomic Nervous System (A.N.S.) in the brain.

As has been told earlier at some length; Anger is a sort of offspring of *Thanatos*. But from the Indian Epics we learn that we should be angry to that extent that will inflict awe but not injury to others, nor it should harm ourselves.

The competitive pattern of life style stimulates intense struggles for reward or status. It calls into play the emotions of Aggressiveness, Fear or Anger. Anger is a natural reaction to Frustration. Basically there is nothing unworthy in Anger itself. It is used only to motivate the wholesome attempts to overcome obstructions that lie in the way of some goal. This Aggression, due to Disappointment or Frustration leads to the development of Anger, associated with *Hate* and *Rage*. The Anger, which produces strong responses in the Autonomic Nervous Systems (A.N.S.) is responsible for congregation of impulses to promote desire to inflict injury on the object of hatred.

Anger is said to be the most serious one out of the six 'Ripus' in the human beings. Ripu (in Sanskrit) means enemy; but if they are controlled in a right manner, these may prove to be friends rather than foes. We cannot possibly live absolutely without these six Ripus, that represents the appetite or passions in us. These are Lust, Anger, Avarice, Delusion, Pride and Envy. (*Kaam, Krodh, Loove, Mohoh, Mada & Matsarya* in Sanskrit). When we set some idea in our brain or make a particular way of life as our habit, we feel uneasy in any other situation that we are in. This Non-adjustability in us provokes us to generate *Hate* for the particular person or situation. Thereafter, if we are not able to compromise, Anger is generated in us. Even in our Indian Epic "SRIMAD BHAGWAD GEETA", it is said in III/31, that, "Rajo-Gunah (over active quality) leads (us) to Lust, which ultimately drives us to *Anger*, which is our acute Enemy."

But how to control ourselves from the clutches of this Anger, once we are in; or how at all to avoid from falling into the clutches of Anger! The common man thinks that the only way to get rid of all this Anger is to give a demonstration of our feelings. But, no; it will become a vicious circle. As we give an expression to our feelings, our environment, be it a person or persons, definitely react to it and give more fuel to the fire. This way, the degree of Anger gets enhanced and it takes the shape of violence culminating in destruction.

How is it, then, possible to quench this Anger? Is it at all possible to control or contain this Anger, once it has grown in us? Before this Anger gets a good get-up on us, is it possible to control it and check it and prevent a disaster? Yes, this is possible, and for that we are to train ourselves.

If we think, that this Anger is born out of our *Ego* to oppose and fight all the ills and irregularities of the world, then we are doomed. Instead, if we think that this Anger is not evolved out of our Own Vital Force and is merely from an outside agent, then we can evict the Anger. This is what the Mother of Pondicherry also thought of. Whenever, we feel that some situation is provoking us to be Angry, immediately we should stand back, look at it very calmly in detached equanimity. If you feel that this situation is coming to you very often, then you should paste these words on a card board and hang it in your living room:

IF YOU ARE ANGRY !
STAND BACK BE CALM &
LOOK IN DETACHED EQUANIMITY.

Practice, what you read on the Card Board, and you will find that you are a changed personality in a fortnight's time.

You have known the possible reasons to become Angry. The adverse circumstances will come, but is it necessary for us to get swayed away by these and get Angry? Yes, sometimes we cannot help it because we are too weak to face these. We think that this Anger is a component part of our own self. Some people are obsessed by their own thoughts. If we think that these evils are all from outside and not originated from our own Inner Vital Force, then these cannot harm us. We will be able to control and contain our Anger. This is what Mother of Pondicherry has told us.

Another way to control Anger is to speak to ourselves, "Keep Quiet". An example will elucidate it. Suppose you have locked the main door of your house and were walking out towards the main gate, but suddenly you became doubtful and walked back to check the main door again. This may continue for several times till you will say, "Enough of it, now keep Quiet". The story may stop then only and you will suppress the incoming Anger.

There are numerous ways to control Anger. We must control Anger, any way, as Anger leads to hatred, delusion, destruction and absolute disintegration of self and others. When we are Angry, we quickly plan out some speech and action and manipulate to make a pulp out of these and impinge on the person or object, we are angry with! The result is a chain reaction of disorder, disaster and destruction.

All these told earlier are the first aids, when we are already in or going to be in, for the battle of Anger. Why not make some preparations so that we may put up a good shield against Anger before it actually grabs us?

Prayers and Aasans for Tension

This subject that I am going to tell you is so vast and arid that I don't venture to deal in details; lest you readers will loose interest in reading it. .But I will tell you something very rare and down to earth things that the readers will definitely get convinced and will gradually start practicing the methods or lessons prescribed, and ultimately will get benefitted.

Choose a place and time where nobody will disturb you absolutely, for at least half an hour or so in a day. Stand with your feet slightly apart and arms hanging by your sides. Close your Eyes and take a deep breath and speak in your mind, "I bring the cosmic Force into my body". Hold your breath and speak to yourself "Give me strength, protection and guidance". Then exhale very slowly. Repeat this process three times. This is a process of PRANAYAM in YOGA. This is one set. If you repeat this 10 times every day, say in the early mornings, then definitely it will show its colours. This Pranayam will not only help to ward away the Anger but will also help in building your mind so strong that you will be able to withstand all circumstances. Many have done it, why not you?

'Prayer' is one of the strongest psychic forces, we have and it is a matter of shame that most of us do not use it to our own betterment. You may think that 'Prayer' is either for the old men and women or for the priests in temples and churches. But you must know that prayer is nothing more than ESP with God. If you do not believe in God, then you may call it the Creator. But Prayer you must do.

This prayer can save us from the clutches of *Mortido*, the destruction force in us. By dint of Prayer and Meditation only we can reach our superconsciousness. By Meditation and Self-Hypnosis, we can achieve complete mental relaxation. By this method, we can build inside us, a direct line with the Creator. Did you not see the difference of talking to a person in a crowd and talking to him on a direct line over the telephone! Nobody disturb you then. You cannot only talk to Him, but you can hear the important instructions from Him also. This Direct Line of Communication is very essential. In a way, if we can 'Turn Inward' and communicate with the HE is us, most of the *Mortido* in us can be controlled. By prayer and meditation much of the psychic energy and the spiritual vibrations are released into the level of the Cosmic Forces. We, then will be able to push our *Ego* out of our way, and will be able to listen to the Inward Message.

In all our religions, it is customary that we speak out some words like "Om" or "Abracadabra" or "Amen" etc. What do the sounds do? Sounds send out vibrations and vibrations make the shape of things. But it is to be kept in mind that these Prayers or Pranayams are to be done in seclusion only as far as is possible. If it is not possible to do it in seclusion, then at least mentally you must detach yourself from the other worldly affairs as is done in Masjids, Mandirs and Churches when we are to pray in congregation.

Out of the Ripus in us function wise, *Anger* is the most precarious one. But others also do harm us, if those are not under our control. We have been condemning all the Ripus all along, specially the *Anger*. Yes, these *Mortidinal* components may harm us profusely. But can we live without these? Imagine yourself, without an iota of *Mortido* in you. You will not be able to mend your pencil with a pen knife. neither you will be able to mince your vegetables for preparing the dishes. The sculptor will not be able to make a statue nor a potter be able to turn out an earthen piece of work. The artisans like, Turner or Carpenter etc. will not be able to cut metal or wood respectively for making utility goods for our daily need. The medical surgeon will not be able to operate upon, say, a tumor in your stomach. These are normal functions which will be disrupted without the excitement of '*Mortido*' in us. But again, the excess of it will also lead us to disaster.

But, what works as an equalizer for the Libido-Mortido imbalance? Prayer is the answer. Prayer, as is told earlier also, is a sort of direct communication with the self in you. I say, self in you, because if I say direct communication with the Creator or God, you may reject the idea. But it is all the same. Because, God is to many, an immaterial aspect which is non-existent, and that we may realise only through our religions idols or prophets or divine apostles and messengers. Prayer, as it sounds, is not so easy either to perform. It is essential for us to clean our body and mind to a considerable extent to be able to indulge ourselves to prayer. Muslims do it in their own way. It is customary that before performing Namaz five times in a day, the parts of the body are cleaned with water which is termed as *Wazu*. In Hindus also, a similar process is in vogue. Hindus are supposed to perform prayer at least two times a day, once at the dawn and another at the dusk. They are supposed to wash their hands and feet, if not the whole body, before starting the prayer. The Muslims believe that the reward on performing Namaz in congregation is twenty seven times powerful as much as on saying it alone. It is customary for the Christians to assemble in a church on every Sunday and pray, as is done on every Friday by the Muslims; Hindus, however, offer prayer separately, except on particular occasions or ceremonies.

Before doing prayer, both the body and the mind should be cleaned up. Cleaning the body is not so very difficult but the whole episode starts afresh for cleaning the mind. To clean the mind, the body culture is a must. The body and the mind are intricately interlaced. This has been told in details in my book "How to be Happy, Healthy and Rich". The first step for cleaning up the body is by Aasana (posture) and Pranayama (regulation, conservation and control of bio-energy, *i.e.*, Prana). Our foremost exponent and compiler of Yoga, Patanjali (BC-200) defined Aasana, as the body pose for steadiness, pleasant and comfortable. It was found by the ancient seers of India even before the Veda Period (BC-5000) that the value of posture as an external aid to the higher purposes of life. These Aasanas and Pranayamas are prelude to the permanent good health (physical and mental) and thus is a prelude to undisturbed meditation.

You must have conjectured that I am heading for Yoga. Various types of misunderstandings have prevailed regarding Yoga, not only in Europe and other continents but most unfortunately in India also to some extent. The misconceptions have frightened many. It is still believed by many, that Yoga is extremely dangerous and thus is intended for only a few who have renounced the world and that it is unsuited to all others except the Hindus. Contrary to this, we find that many of the exponents of Yoga, were married and maintained their families happily. As a matter of fact, the Muslims and the Christians too, make some such poses of the body as is required for Yoga by us. Here, our ultimate aim is Prayer, a method for the direct communication with the Self; the innerself. But, for the approach to prayer, we have to pass through a few simple stages like Asana, Pranayama etc. which are part of Yoga. And Yoga represents the way of life which endows perfect health - physical, mental, moral and spiritual.

Let us see how Yoga helps us to reach that stage which enables us to perform our prayers. When Yoga is interpreted, it represents the way of life which endows perfect health. The whole process of Yoga is splitted up into these following sections:

(a) Yama and Niyama.

(b) Aasana,

(c) Pranayama,

(d) Pratihara,

(e) Dharana and Dhyana, and lastly

(f) Samadhi.

For the common man to be able to pray, it is not absolutely necessary to strictly follow all the above six stages preliminary to Yoga. Of all, Aasana is a must, followed by Dharana (concentration) and then Dhyana (meditation). The ultimate, is Meditation. There is a serenity that comes from Meditation, we cannot get it in any other way.

A British Author J.I. Wedgwood defined "Meditation as an endeavour to bring into waking consciousness, the mind in its normal state of activity. Some realization of the superconsciousness."

Meditation lets us to visualize the 'Truth' inside ourselves. In the Upanisads, it is written "What a man thinks on, he becomes." This thinking is not any casual thinking or well wishing. It is visualization through Meditation. Problems are there and will be, but know it for all that there is no problem that does not come accompanied by a solution. Rather, somebody told that "Problems are born with solutions." And it is we who are to unfold the solutions through Meditation only.

As told earlier, if our aim of Meditation is to achieve the stage which enables us to become apt for prayer only, then it is not necessary to go through all these stages of Yoga. If we strictly follow the Yoga ideal, our perfect health is assured. But our aim, now, is prayer.

For the common man, to move through all the processes of Yoga, may not be impossible either because so many people have already practiced or are practicing the same. To perform all the feats of Yoga by our own self is neither practicable nor feasible. But to practice Dhyana after Dharana is rather simple and the common man may achieve success if he tries at it very sincerely, for a couple of months or so.

Meditation

If you are interested to know and practice the complete course of Yoga, you may buy a book on Yoga and start practicing Yoga under the guidance of a Guru.

But here, I may help you only to do the Meditation after concentration; by giving you some simple methods of performances as below:

1. Leave your bed before Sunrise.
2. Complete your morning performances.
3. Select a suitable quiet place which should be airy, if possible.
4. Sit in your Sukhasan with your spine absolutely straight.
5. Close your Eyes and try to think about nothing (This is the most difficult part).
6. Utter the Word 'Om', in full but subdued voice stretching it every time like Omm.....m.....m, Om.....m.....m.....m.....m".
7. Then after a few minutes, open your Eyes. Light a candle (or a paraffin stick) before you.
8. Stare at the flame and utter the word 'Om' as previously done, for quite a few minutes, till you see the flame taking different shapes and colour.

During all these processes, you are to think about nothing. But in the beginning it will be very difficult. At least I had a lot of difficulties for quite a few weeks, till it was all very soothing.

If you are convinced now about what has been told, and got interested in it, I may tell you a more detailed and intricate method for meditation. As a matter of fact, there are many of them; but I will tell you a simple but firm way to practice Meditation.

(1) Sit upright in Sukhasan as told earlier.

(2) Bend your head slightly down, exhale all air from your lungs.

(3) Breathe in very slowly as you gradually pull your body and concentrate all your energies at a point at the centre of your forehead.

(4) Keep your eyes closed and palms folded and count in your mind from one to twenty very slowly.

(5) If you do not want to keep your eyes closed you may continue looking at the flame of the candle.

(6) You will, after about twenty minutes, see the flame, miraculously changing colour and shape.

(7) You are then in Meditation.

(8) After a couple of months exercise, you will see that you will take even less time to reach this stage.

(9) Now you are in your Aura. You can do miracles. You can do so many feats; plan something, ask for something and achieve something.

(10) All these will be possible if you have done all these feats sincerely and seriously.

Faith, Prayer & Miracle

It is seen that people in all the religions pray. But it is to be seen, as to how many of us pray sincerely and seriously? You can pray, either in congregation or in seclusion, but in all the cases, you are to be sincere and serious. Do not think that Prayer is for old ladies or the priests only. You have to be in a trance, you have to be in your Aura through meditation. Prior to Prayer, you are to prepare yourself through Meditation. Since you are in meditation, you are in direct line with the Cosmic Force.

The Preliminary criterion revolves around Faith. But faith in whom? The common man does not believe in God and hence to have faith in Him does not arise. If you cannot have faith in anybody then try to have faith in yourself. It will work. The common man cannot have any faith in an imaginary body which he thinks, does not exist. To him, God is an abstract thing. It is a long process, first to convince a person about the existence of God and then create faith in Him. We start concentrating on the material objects around Him, *viz.* the Earth, the Sun, the Moon, the Wind, the Plants and the Plantations. These inanimate bodies are Truth only, they exist very well and there is no question of denying their existence. We should create Love for these things first. When Love is imbibed in these things, our half the battle is won. These things must have been created somehow and by somebody. Who is that body? Who is that person? Whoever He may be, if these things are Truth, then the existence of the Creator of these things is also Truth. If we agree, we should have faith in Him.

Then gradually turn your mind inward. This is done by Self Hypnosis. And Self Hypnosis is possible by Meditation only. Thereby, you create a direct line with the 'Creator'. A great majority of men, except, probably, those who are masochists love themselves and have faith in themselves only. This faith is not for any particular goal. This faith is a sort of complete surrender.

You have seen that we developed our faith in the Creator of the objects around us. And we ourselves are also created by the same Creator. Then, when we have faith in the Creator for objects around us, we being one of those objects, we create faith in us also.

By Meditation we are in a trance and are on the Direct Line with the Cosmic Forces, then by creating Faith in us, means creating Faith in God. At this the second half of the battle is also won. When this state of mind is reached, if you think of something very seriously and sincerely then you will surely achieve that thing.

These prayer sessions should be sincere but not loud or lengthy or emotional. Of course, you may hymn loudly but with subdued voice. Indians shout and at times put their prayers through loud speakers, as if God is deaf.

Of course, vibrations from sound do create patterns and patterns form designs and it is from these designs the objects are formed into beings. Have you heard the forceful Tantric (Indian), Mantras (Hymns) like "Om, Hring, Shring etc." It is said that they are very forceful.

Problem Solved by Prayer

If you have a problem, then sit very comfortably in meditation for sometime in a secluded place, and then open out your problem to the Creator, privately as you talk to your brother or father. Do not shout or get emotional. Your talk should not be lengthy either, but you should be very sincere. You will definitely be guided and if the thing you want is within your reasonable range, then you will surely get it. You will definitely win and get benefitted.

You yourself, can draw a long list from your experience or the experiences of your grand mother when prayers were rewarded. But I shall give you a few examples from my own experience.

As far as I remember, it was the mid 70's, when a Faith Healer had come to Delhi from the South of India. A meeting was called in a Church Court Yard where several hundred men and women gathered to witness his feats. The person was an Indian Christian from a Church in South India. I had seen many miracles by him that afternoon. But, one I remember vividly. A North Indian couple had come with their 15 year old daughter who could not walk due to some defect in her right leg. She had to be carried on the platform and to be laid on a raised bed. The priest started chanting prayers for about twenty minutes very seriously and sincerely, asking God to cure the girl and went on thanking Him in advance for it. Then after sometime, he asked the girl's parents to tell the child to walk. To my astonishment, I saw her walking and then after that she went back to her seat very comfortably. Is it not a miracle of Prayer?

On some other occasion, I had gone to Mount Abu with my sister-in-law and her husband. When we were stranded there, my prayers were complied with and we were saved. While coming down from Mount Abu in a pre-paid Taxi, the steering wheel became free and we got panicky. I immediately switched over to the cosmic force and got enough courage and directions from Him. Had I not compelled the driver to put the car to a dead halt, we should have been in the deep pits ahead. We had to reach the Udaipur Railway Station by 2.00 P.M. from where we had already booked our berths for Delhi. We tried to stop many taxis and private cars. Those were either overloaded or they simply refused us for a lift. We all three sat on the side of the rocky mountain, hungry and exhausted, that afternoon. I continued my prayers sincerely and deeply. I, then mustered courage to stand almost at the middle of the road to stop some vehicle. To my amazement, I saw a bus slowing down, which contained packed up passengers from Switzerland. As if God had sent these people to us; they made room for us to sit and were very hospitable to us. Had we not got that bus, we did not know what would have been our condition in that wilderness and darkness.

Going back a few years hence, I had another miraculous experience. As the motor garage of our newly constructed house was lying vacant, it was rented out. But, when I purchased a car for myself, I asked the tenant to vacate. He played lot of tricks for not vacating the premises. When all the hearings in the Court went in favour of the tenant, I started praying daily, and praying very sincerely, as there was no other alternative to it. As directed by my Lord Krishna, I withdrew the case from the Court and coaxed them to promise me that they would handover the keys to me. Apprehending that they may ultimately refuse the keys, on the final day, before going to the party to get back the keys, I sat down for deep meditation in the afternoon and prayed to my Lord Krishna that my wishes be fulfilled. My prayer was heeded to and I got the keys of my garage.

Yet, another true incident, I am to relate to you for you to believe that sincere prayer is answered with a solution. This time it was my wife who prayed. The owner of the ground floor of the building in which we recently purchased a flat on the first floor in Calcutta, started a catering restaurant. We had a lot of inconveniences, *viz.,* smoke, smell and sound nuisance throughout the day till eleven in the Night. Our repeated requests to stop or minimise these nuisances, were all futile. Then my wife, who is a staunch believer in Lord Krishna, started praying for hours very sincerely for help. After a few months, we found that the owner of the restaurant closed down his business with an idea to open a different type of business there.

Now, you have seen, how we can change our *Libido* to win over our *Mortido* to save our soul. The *Love* element in us if charged and if we can bring Faith in ourselves first, being sincere and truthful, and then gradually extend it further and bridge a direct line with the Cosmic Force, ultimately big problems can be solved in the ways we want. Biographies of Sri Rama Krishna Paramhansa, Swami Vivekananda, Sri Aurobindo and Mother of Pondicherry reveal that they also had done many extra-ordinary deeds by the methods mentioned above.

In all the cases, it is not necessary to be present at the site of the activity. As a matter of fact, Rishi Aurobindo, during his stay in Jail or in the Aurovilley Ashram, carried on so many activities sitting miles away only by his mental powers, which he developed by Yoga and Meditation. More details will be found in the least Chapter of this Book.

There is an advice for the young men and women in the middle age group (30 - 40 years of age). It is high time that they should start Yoga and then pray through Meditation if they had not started earlier.

This book is not meant to coach them for Yoga or Meditation or Self Hypnosis, but only to inspire them for these.

Enough has been told to do some exercise to have control over our mind so that if we can "catch them young", then the end product will be a *Libido* oriented personnel. If we have not thought over the aspect till we are 40 or 50 years of age, then it will be too late. We will then emerge as sophisticated hooligans.

We are to take a pledge that we shall have to save this world from a catastrophy. As we are also one of the members of this world we shall have to save ourselves first.

4
SEX

The very word *Sex* allures us so much that we immediately get proned to switch over to the exclusive topics of *Sex*, so that we may hear or see more and more of it to enable us to be in the arena. Think for a moment, why does it happen like this? Is it because, the subject is of *Sex*, that ultimately culminates in "Orgasm"? And then again, what is 'Orgasm"? How the Orgasm is originated and developed? What is the ultimate goal of the 'Orgasm"? Does the story stop at Orgasm, or it percolates further to open another new chapter? Attempts will be made to meet all the answers in this Chapter.

Talking of the impact of the word *Sex*, let us see, how a gentleman made a mess of the term *Sex* and how he was exasperating to get out of the quagmire, as if. The man narrated the story and you will get to know from the horse's mouth.

"One who has a dog, calls him Johny, Tiger or Puppy. But, I call mine *Sex*. He is a great pal to me. But it caused me tremendous embarrassment, when I went to the Corporation Office, to renew his 'Dog Licence'. I told the clerk, that I would like a licence for '*Sex*'. He said, "I like one too!" "But, this is a 'Dog'," I said. He then said, that he did not care what she looked like. I then said, "you do not understand, I had *Sex*, since I was nine years old." At that he wrinkled, and said, "You must have been quite a kid then, Isn't it?"

Then after a year or so, when I got married, and went on my 'honeymoon', I took the Dog with me. I told the hotel manager that I wanted a room for my wife and me and a special room for '*Sex*'. At that, he said, "you do not need a special room, as long as you pay your bill, and we do not care what you do!" I got embarrassed and said, "Look, you do not seem to understand, '*Sex*' keeps me awake at night. The manager said, "Funny man, I have the same problem."

A few years later, when my wife and I got separated, I went to the Court, to fight for custody of the dog. I said, "your Honour, I had '*Sex*', before I was married, and that after I was married, "*Sex*' left me." He said, "Me too, gentleman."

Then, after all that, last night *Sex* ran off again. I spent hours looking around for him in the streets. A policeman came over to me and asked me, "What are you doing in the dark alley, at 3.00 O'Clock, in the morning?" I said, "I was looking for *Sex*. No sooner he heard me saying this, the policeman chased me, and I somehow managed to save myself from his clutches."

You have seen the impact of the word *Sex*. Let us see, what then *Sex* is. As is generally defined, *Sex* is the characteristic distinction between the male and the female, basically it is the distinction between the organisms that produces 'Eggs' and that produces the 'Sperm Cells', thereby signifying the process of reproduction.

In Botany the nomenclature for these terms are slightly varied. Ultimately, it is a process of procreation, by the Union of male and the female genital organs, by which the orgasmic pleasure and satisfaction is also evolved.

By the words, "having *Sex*", means, to have *Sexual* intercourse between two bodies, generally the male and the female with the help of the respective genital organs.

But, here again, by going through all the findings of the psychological experts it can be said, that *Sex* is a sort of 'Orgasm' produced by the mental association of a person with another person or a thing associated with that person, accompanied with acute physical and mental activities. In the particular cases of the union of a male and a female, it causes a strong Sexual feeling, resulting in secretion of fluids of the sex organs of both culminating in ecstasy and intense pleasure.

The Origin of Orgasm

This pleasure is termed as 'Orgasm'. To understand 'Orgasm', the acute ecstasy and the feeling of intense pleasure, we are to understand, as to, which parts of the brain are directly and indirectly responsible for this feeling. I could not pin point those parts that are responsible for this feeling in the brain, nor the half a dozen medical practitioners whom I consulted could give me a satisfactory answer. The information collected by me lead me to conclude that more research on the subject may one day reveal the secret of the amazing game culminating in orgasm. But, for our discussions, here, we may dwell upon a few glands in the body.

Pituitary Gland is a pea-sized gland which lies in the small hollow in the skull just behind the top of the nose at the eye level and is attached by a thin stalk to the Hypothalamus which is almost at the base of the brain. Out of the two basic lobes, the frontal lobe of the pituitary produces six types of hormones. Out of these six, the Gonadotropic Hormones stimulate and help the production of the *Sex* hormones in the ovaries and testicles.

Now that the Pituitary Gland has an edge over the control of the six hormones and is attached to the Hypothalamus let us see what part of the Hypothalamus and also the Thalamus play in affecting the Sexual activities.

The Gland Thalamus is a mass of grey matter in two egg shaped bodies near the base of the cerebrum, bounding and projecting into the third ventricle. It consists of a number of distinct nuclii, many of which serve as relay stations for the incoming sensory impulses, except those of the sense of smell. The impulses converge on the Thalamus and thereafter are relayed to the cerebral cortex (90% of nerve cells). The Gland Hypothalamus is situated below the Thalamus. It contains centres for regulation of the body temperature, blood pressure

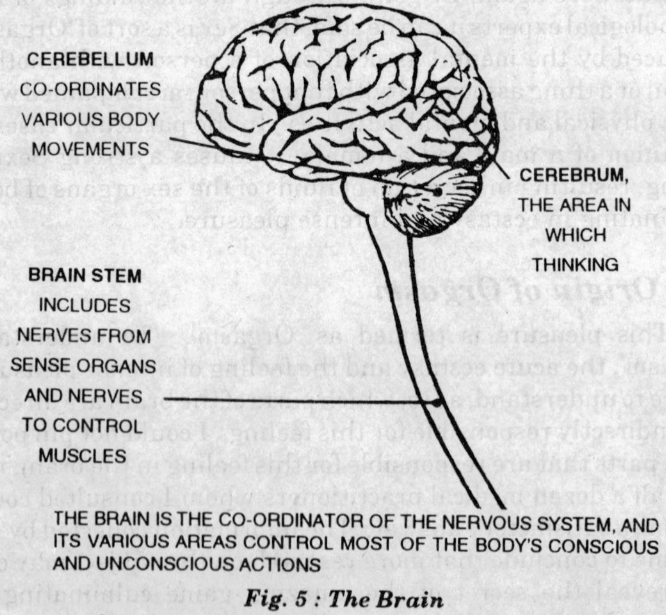

Fig. 5 : The Brain

and it also regulates the drives of Hunger, Thrust and *Sex*. In addition it is also the source of "Emotional Reactions."

These three Glands are primarily responsible for sexual arousement and orgasm. But there may be other parts in the Cerebrum and Cerebellum which contribute to this function. Both the sex glands of the male and the female are energised or activated to complete the ceremony. Subsequent secondary spots which are responsible for the production and perception of orgasm are yet to be known, perhaps researches may reveal that in the near future. Having known the functions of the Pituitary, Thalamus and Hypothalamus glands, we can frame an idea that these are the only primary glands that are responsible for the "sexual arousement and orgasm."

It is now our prime look-out that these basic glands are groomed correctly so that we can have more pleasure and ecstasy in our life time. This is possible, to much extent by practising "Dhyanasan" and other suitable Aasans of Yoga and adopting correct food habits also.

What is Sex?

Before going into details, regarding, what *Sex* is for a common man, let us digress a bit to excavate the birth of *Sex*. Looking back to Fig. 3 again, we find that the *ID* we have from our childhood can be splitted into two entities, *viz.*, *Libido* and *Mortido*. The *Libido*, the *Love* Element in us is for creation and *Mortido*, the Hate element is for destruction. But this *Love* element again has dual functions (as was told earlier). It is partially creative and partially destructive. If it would have been all creative, then we would not have existed as we are now. You may understand it better if you take the example of gold. It is very difficult to give shape and construct and fabricate beautiful objects out of pure gold till we mix some other harder metal to facilitate giving a form and make good use of the gold. Similarly, a little bit of hate element is necessary to make use of the *Libido*. But the extreme on either side will be harmful.

For example, very few people who are purely *Libidinal*, (*i.e.*, more of *Love* Element), exist in this world. Some Vice, some Hatred, some Jealousy, some Anger, some Envy is necessary to live our lives, as we do. On the other hand, if we have more of

Hate element in us and very little of *Love*, then we not only will try to destroy the world, but we ultimately may destroy ourselves also.

In our hindu mythology, God lives in three Phases. God has three different types of powers in Him. We have, *Brahma*, the Creator; *Vishnu*, the maintainer; *Maheshwar*, the destructor. It is said that the powers of all the three phases of God are utilized rightly for maintenance of the Universe, whether they are animate or inanimate.

The Creator *Brahma* rules the domain of the Cosmic Energy, the eternal life element. The Cosmic Energy of the universe is enormous and is a Constant. All sorts of creations are nothing but transformations of this Energy. The father and the mother are giving birth to a child. But it is a sort of transformation only. The father and mother are not immortal. The child is there as a transformation of the parents.

The second part of God is *Vishnu*, the maintainer. Every object animate or inanimate has got a normal life span that is designed by *Lord Vishnu*.

The Scholars of Chemistry know that every atom is bound by a force and they rotate in their particular orbits for a definite length of period till some of them are disturbed by external excitement. Then what happens? When the life of the element is complete, does it get perished? No, it gets transformed. My aim is not to disgress towards Physics or Chemistry but to impress upon you that it is not necessary for all things to continue its life for an eternal time. Even the tiniest particle on earth (atom) may change or transform if excited by some external agents. In their cases the electromagnetic urge is responsible for the change. This is the law of nature. Students of Chemistry must be familiar with the terms as 'Affinity, Reaction, Transformation, Catalytic Agent' and so on. In our own life also, we meet similar situations.

When a boy meets a girl and a particular sensation is evolved in them, they react to it and are attracted to each other. This they call as '*Love*'. A man meets another man of the same tune or frequency (mental), and there is a similar reaction and they also love each other. But as Freud opines every *Love* has a force of *Sex* behind it. *Love* & *Sex* are two independent as well as two inter-dependent aspects, as if, one is the catalytic agent of the other. When we are in *Love*, we do not know that the driving force is *Sex*. Similarly, when we are in the domain of *Sex*, we do not know that it is the mutual *Love*, that is responsible for the stage of *Sex*. *Sex* is not always to be taken in the crude sense as the common man thinks. This is somewhat similar to the electronic force in atoms.

Plants and Animals

Homosapiens are born, grow and are ultimately perished. Similarly, all other creatures like various animals, birds and fishes etc. have definite life spans. Some live for 10/20 years, some for 40/60 years and again some for several hundred years also. They all have to die ultimately. They do perish after a scheduled period destined for the species. Some plants like seasonal flowers or seasonal vegetables and cereals are perished after a few months only. All of them have got definite life span.

Geologists and astronomers calculated the age of the Earth as between 3440 and 4500 millions of years. When the Earth gradually cooled down there was a spontaneous generation of life. Life is mysterious and it is assumed that many millions of years ago, life just came in existence in water in a speck of *Protoplasm,* which as Huxley defined it, is the actual living substance in plants and animals. According to fossil records, life seems to be present about 600 million years ago in the form of bacteria, fungi, blue green algae and some primitive invertebrates. Again, the structural similarities of roots, stems, leaves, flowers, and other morphologic characters among certain groups of plants and the bones and other organs among certain groups of animals, and the successive stages in the development of such organs from simpler to more complex forms, evidently show the evolutionary tendencies of plants and animals towards perfection.

The study of the nature and development of the Embryo in the Homosapiens reveal a great resemblance among certain groups of plants and animals. The development indicates the evolutionary changes that has taken place through the successive stages. Embryo is the earliest stage of development in the womb. In us the embryonic period is held to extend from the time of the conception to about 06-12 weeks. The foetal stage then follows. (Foetal means, pertaining to Foetus, the unborn baby, after the second month following conception). In all cases it is revealed that one thing is common to the plants and animals is that the embryo develops from the egg cell or the ovum.

There is a close similarity between the fertilization of animals and the plants. But, there are dissimilarities also. In the animals, the male meets the females, implants the spermatoza and the ovam is fertilized to give birth to an offspring. This is true with the Homosapiens, as well as the lower grades of other animals. But with the plants this is not always so. With the plants there are three principal methods of reproduction, *viz:*

(a) Sexual

(b) A - Sexual

(c) Vegetative

(d) Special Modes of Reproduction

In Sexual reproduction, like that of animals and of higher forms of plant life, the pairing gametes are male and female. The union of dissimilar gametes in plants is known as fertilization. The female gamete in them is much larger but are stationary and passive (almost like those in animals) and is called egg-cell or ovum. The female reproductive units in the flowering plant, is the gamete which is called the egg cell or the ovum of the embryo sac within the Ovule, and the male reproductive unit of the flowering plant is the gamete of the Pollen Tube.

In 1694, Camerarius established for the first time, the fact that Pollination is essential for the production of the seed and thus proved the sexuality in plants. Pollination is the transference of pollen grains from another flower to the stigma of the same flower or from another flower of the same plant, often through various agencies such as wind, insects etc.

From 1764 to 1806 Koelreuter worked in Berlin and pollinated some 300 and odd flowers of different species. By microscopic examination of the pollen grains on the stigma, he noticed that some oily substance oozed out of the grains and mixed with the oil secreted by the stigma, worked down into the style and entered into the ovary and thereby producing an embryo.

Pollination of the flowering plants are by the wind as well as by the insects. The insects are attracted by the colour and the fragrance of the flowers and hence come over to sit on the flowers to collect and enjoy the honey from the flowers.

The readers might have understood the utility of the beautiful colour and fragrance of the flowers. Both of these are essential for the reproduction of the flowering plants. In the animals, one partner attracts the other, so that they may get enough excitement to enable them to unite and cause the union of the spermatoza and the ova for reproduction. Whether, it is the human beings or the animals, the male members are more robust and healthy. Generally, the male members have the first approach. It is the peacocks who spread their colourful wings and dance before the peahens to attract and seduce them for mating. In human beings, it is slightly different. The females coaxe the males in passive ways by displaying their female forms, looks, and gait. The male show their chivalry, mettle and efficacy to win the heart of the female who has already been able to throw her Cupids towards the male.

Unlike plants, animals, reproduce in a definite mode, *i.e.*, Sexual, (as compared to 4 modes for plants). Animals follow the "Sexual Mode" like human beings. Both the males implant their Spermatoza on to the ova of the female and the transformation gives rise to the birth of a baby mostly of the feature and character of the parents (the male and the female). I said mostly, because the influence of the environment is also there to shape the intelligence of the child.

Sir Francis Galton (1869), Drs. A.F. Tredgold, Terman, Cox and Hollingworth made intensive studies. We find from these that the environment has more influence on 'Shaping the body of the child than the heredity. But heredity has got influence in shaping the intelligence of the child.

Dr. Bentley Glass, again, from his numerous experiments and researches found that the number of possible combinations of the offspring, resulting from the union of the human egg and the spermatoza to be 281, 474, 967, 710, 656.

Women's Status and Trait

Regarding the female form, I can quote one episode from my life. In 1980 when I was travelling towards Trivandrum on my Bharat Darshan (Tour of India), after my retirement from the services, one afternoon, I had the occasion to talk with a group of young bank officers—4 males and 2 females, in the compartment in a train. I sketched out a few line diagrams and handed over one sketch to each officer, and requested them to grade those according to the attractiveness of those figures. To my amazement, the result was as depicted below:-

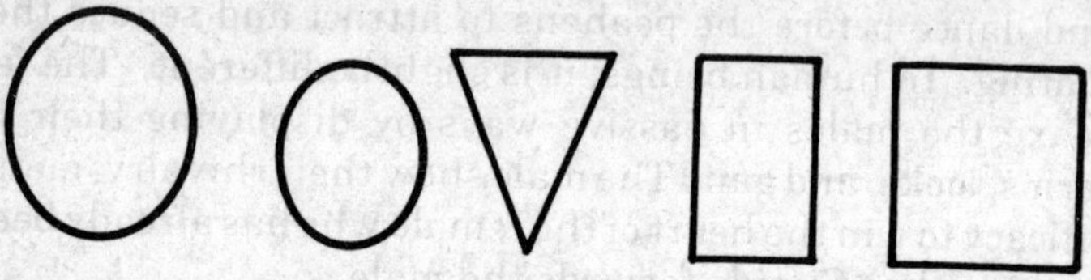

A	1	2	3	4	5
B	1	3	2	4	5
C	1	3	2	4	5
D	2	3	1	5	4
E	1	2	3	4	5
F	1	2	3	5	4

Fig. 6

By and large, the maximum score was for the Fig. No.1, then for No. 2 and No. 3 and so on. This proved that the curvacious figure of the female like those is the sketch is most appealing to the eyes of all.

It is an established fact that women are weaker sex of the two, and meek also. But that does not mean that they are inferior to men, in any respect. Women excel men in many aspects. The most salient aspect is that their form and texture are made of such material that they are more appealing specially to the opposite sex. Their flesh has softer tissues containing more of fat hence their skin is softer and the skin is devoid of hairs also. The artists will agree with me, if I say that the eyes and the texture of women are both appealing to the eyes more than those of men. They are quickwitted but more polished than men. For intricate jobs, and complicated problems, men cannot overthrow them out. Hence in our vedic days, women were given a higher status than men.

Now, the time has come again, that women should be given ample opportunities to contribute more to the society. I do not say equal opportunity. In some fields women may excel men. Hence, in those fields, they should be allowed ample opportunities to contribute to the society to the best of their abilities.

The females are lucky enough not to suffer from sex linked diseases like baldness, haemophillia or colour blindness. In the reproductive system, there is a basic anamoly. The male spermatozoa contains one X and one Y chromosome, whereas the female ova or the egg cell, contains two X chromosomes. You should know that chromosomes are rods or thread like things occurring in pairs in cell-nucleus and carrying genes; and gene is the factor in the germ cell causing development of the inherited characteristic.

In the human species, there are 22 pairs of chromosomes plus two sex determiners, totalling 46 in number.

When an X chromosome unites with an Y chromosome, the result is a male baby, whereas if an X chromosome unites with another X chromosome, the result is a female baby. One thing is to be noted in this context, it is the male member who is responsible for creating a male baby and not the female member. Due to ignorance in our society, the groom's mother blames the

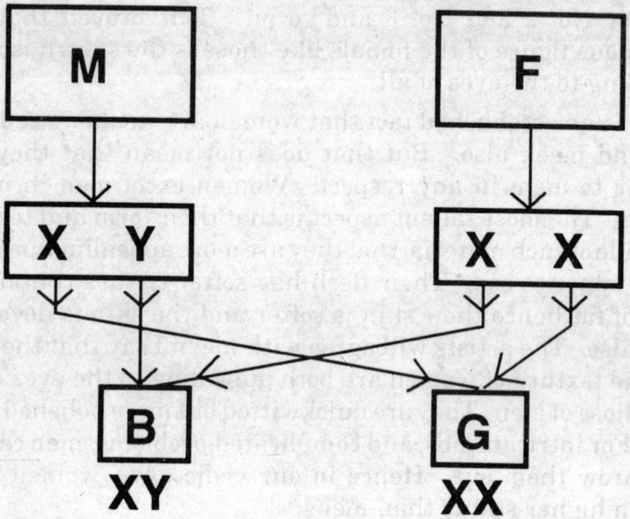

Fig. 7

bride only for being unable to give birth to a male child. Let us understand what gene is. It is the factor in the germ cell causing the development of the inherited characteristics of the baby born. According to the genetic theory of sex linked traits, the genes responsible for the sex linked diseases are located in the sex determining chromosome X only. But when that X chromosome comes in contact with Y chromosome, the sex linked diseases like baldness, haemophilia or colour blindness will show up in the male offspring only and not in the female baby. But, amazingly, if the same X chromosome containing some sex linked diseases, meets with another healthy X chromosome (either from the male or the female) then the tendency is, that X chromosome cancels out the disease. The resulting female baby (XX) will not inherit that sex linked disease. The irregularities in these findings are very rare. Hence, in female members, baldness etc. are also very rare. Nature has again saved the women from being unfortunate. Women then, are again blessed by the nature, in the sexual maturity in early childhood. The girl child starts maturing sexually at an early age as of 9 years whereas a boy matures at the age of 13 years. This is as if women are burning their candles on the both ends and get extinguished early.

With all that is said and done, the female members, enjoy sexual maturity at an early stage, but enjoy their sex life for a shorter period than the males. Men are capable of enjoying sex from the age of 14 to 70 years or more, but for women this is from the age of 12 to 40 years in general. That is women enjoy their sex life for a period, less than half of that of men. Why not the females be given more opportunities to enjoy life during this shorter period and also to contribute more to the society?

DNA and RNA in Chromosomes

As has been told earlier, homosapiens give birth to off springs due to the union of X or Y chromosomes from the male spermatozoa and the X or X chromosomes from the female ova. These chromosomes carry the genes (elementary units of heredity). Heredity trait, is the totality of the characteristics transmitted from the parents to the off springs, be it the plant or the animals (including human beings). The transmission of genetic characteristics is a function of chromosomes and genes, whether contained in the spermatozoa of men or ova of women.

All living objects (plants and animals) grow. Certain non-living bodies, as they are termed as, like crystals, also grow. But this growth is external, whereas the living bodies grow internally. The plants and animals possess the power to reproduce periodically giving rise to off springs of the same kind. But the non-living objects breakdown mechanically into a number of irregular parts.

The DNA and RNA in plants and animals are well known to the students of Botany and Biology. As for the DNA and RNA, they may be called as "Close Chemical Relatives."

J.B. Watson (1878-1958) and Crick, investigating the Neucleic Acids, proposed a 'Double Helix Model' of DNA molecules, which are composed of substructures of Phosphates, Bases and Sugars which determine the genetic information carried by the chromosomes and regulates all the metabolism. Metabolism means physico-chemical changes in the living organism (*i.e.*, Catabolism and Anabolism). This metabolism is an essential feature for the growth of the body.

The Riboneucleic Acid or RNA is a sort of 'Giant Protein Molecule' in the cell nuclii, which is believed to act as messenger to transfer agents in the genetic development of the new organism. Where as the DNA of the Deoxy-rebonucleic Acid functions for regulating the metabolism of the body as is told earlier.

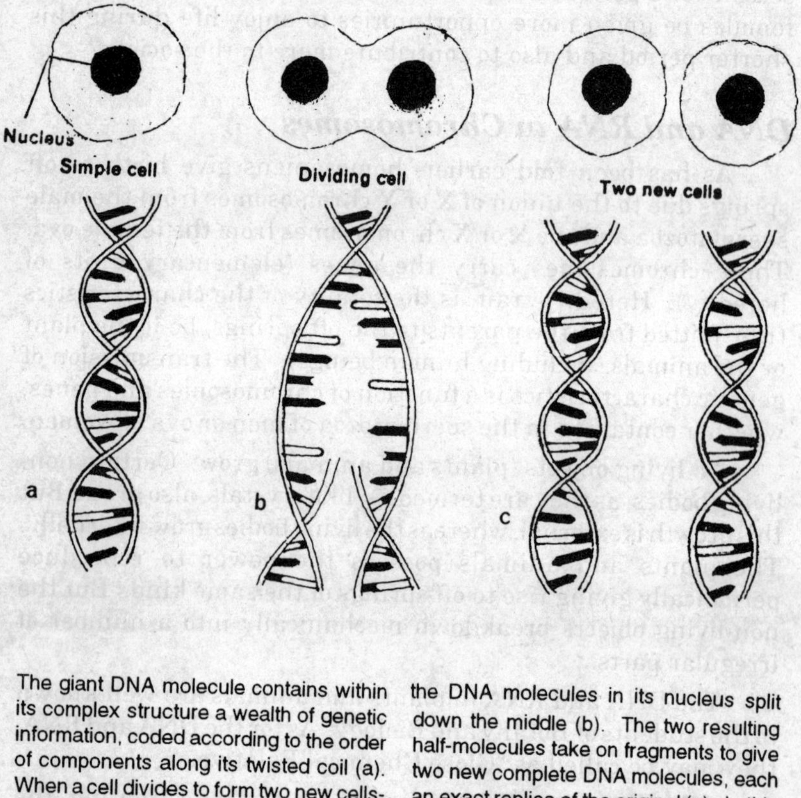

The giant DNA molecule contains within its complex structure a wealth of genetic information, coded according to the order of components along its twisted coil (a). When a cell divides to form two new cells-the normal method of cell reproduction-the DNA molecules in its nucleus split down the middle (b). The two resulting half-molecules take on fragments to give two new complete DNA molecules, each an exact replica of the original (c). In this way, genetic instructions are passed on.

Fig. 8. : The DNA and the RNA

The DNA and RNA are equally effective for the plants as well as animals. But for the objects other than plants and animals, which are called the non-living objects, the scientists are of the opinion that they also grow and live but in a different pattern.

The Miracle of Progeny

Progeny, the birth of an offspring or a baby, is really a miracle. From an infinitesimal particle of chromosome on a base of an ova or the egg, is transformed into an offspring, generally, very near to the kind of the characters of the both, be it a plant or an animal. Is it not a miracle?

I shall try to bring home the salient features and the complicated affairs in a way, only the common reader will understand and enjoy. As the readers will be more interested to know, how our babies are born, I shall concentrate more on the progeny of the human race and not the plants. As told earlier also, though the plants progeny differs in many cases but the common one is the sexual reproduction. Hence let us concentrate on this type of the reproduction only of the human beings.

Men are mature enough to germinate as early as at the age of 10, when most of them start ejaculating, but the sperms are mature enough for reproduction at about the age of 14 only. Whereas the women start evoluting mostly from the age of 9, but are ready to bear a mature child at the age of 12 only. This adolescent periods for both the boys and the girls are in a way precarious. The awareness of the youth starts growing and thus they become frolic and adventurous. The secondary sex characteristics are developed at the advent of puberty only, which becomes difficult for them to conceal, whether it is a boy or a girl. They become emotional and most of them turn exhibitionists also. Both the male and female develop natural sexual urge and the most of them are prone to satisfy the same. This is the time for them to restrain and divert their energies into other creative activities. These adolescents should inculcate the habit of reading profusely, also outside their course of regular studies; but they should be selective not to read books which lead to sexual excitement.

Jean Piaget (1896-1980), a Swiss psychologist, during his research, regarding the cognitive developments of a child, related to thinking, put forward four fundamental stages:

(a) From birth to 2 years.

(b) From the age of of 2 to 7 years.

(c) From the age of 7 to 11 years.

(d) From the age of 11 years and after.

(a) During the first stage the child learns about the objects around him and about time and space.

(b) In the second period of the child, he can represent symbolically and can conceive images of the objects, even in the absence of the objects.

(c) In the third stage, the child is closely tied to the objects and events that are present and masters the conception of mass, length and volume etc. He also becomes less egocentric.

(d) Lastly, during the fourth stage he becomes capable of reasoning, abstracting and thinking hypothetically also.

If the parents are groomed in these concepts, then the child will have less misunderstandings and misconceptions; he thereby can grow into a mature personality.

Generally, it is seen that the child, upto the age of 8 or 9 years (boys as well as the girls), are more attached to their parents. Then during the age of 9 to 11 years, they gradually get more detached, from the parents and start making friends with persons of their own sex, instead. This homosexual behaviour is perfectly natural and normal at this stage. (Homosexual attitude means the inclination of a person to get attached to a member of his own sex and age). This is a sort of 'Repressed Desire' towards a member of the opposite sex). This transition period was obvious and inevitable for the child to compensate the loss of the emotional bondage of their parents. But if this is not checked, and is allowed to continue, then what emerges is, the 'Adult Homo-Sexual'. This will be dealt with at a later stage in this book. Thereafter, from the age of 11 to 12 years, about 1/3rd of them feel more comfortable with the companion of the opposite sex.

At this age the remaining boys and girls do not fall in love with members of the opposite sex. The reason is, that the girls, due to their strong feelings of rivalry with boys, may be unable to fall in love with them, and the boys again for their strong fixation with their mothers, (Oedepus complex as it is called); may be unable to fall in love with any other female member until their mothers either die or get dissociated with them due to any family circumstances. The remaining boys may develop suspicion for the girls and thus they refrain from falling in love with the girls. In this precarious period from the period of 12 to 20 years, the boys and girls may regress to homo-sexual love vigorously. They become vinous to this uncouth homo-sexual activity.

Lot of human misery and despair can be eliminated if the young boys and girls get help from the society in combating this menace. If our society starts realising this abnormal behaviour of homo-sexuality, a sign of immorality and hold a taboo against this practice, and declare it as a social evil and as a punishable offence then only the picture of the present society may change.

Then a couple of years hence, gradually they develop more intimate relations with the companions of the opposite sex and develop real love. The initial intimacy develops into sexual desire. Finally, the normal sexual development occurs and the deepest emotion of love is bestowed on one person, about the same age but of the opposite sex.

John Broadus Watson (1878-1958), the great American Behavioural Psychologist, called it as love.

Finally, may I add, that the "Normal Sexual Development" occurs when the love object or person who inspite of the deepest emotion of love comes to be the only one person of the opposite sex and of about the same age.

General Excitement and Sexual Emotion

At birth, we had two salient emotions; pain and pleasure. The feeling of pain was experienced when we used to have discomfort of any sort, and that of pleasure when either our demands and aspirations were met with satisfactorily, either by material gain or by the feeling of love. For a child, the sexual love is not as strong as that of sensuous gratification. All this is true, upto puberty. Thereafter, the excitement of love, activates the sex glands and the hormones are released by the process, and activates the Adrenaline Glands, which leads to the feeling of Orgasm in the brain which irrigates the whole body with a gush of blood. The heart beats are enhanced, the blood pressure increases and a state of ecstasy is achieved.

According to Dr. Kothari there are certain 'G' points in the body which when stimulated, in the male or the female body, the sensory nerves are activated. As to which particular parts are responsible for the production or orgasm is still a mystery. Yet, it is said, that when the messages reach the Thalamus, some nuclei are activated and the chemical, Adrenaline is discharged from the Adrenaline Gland, which is, to much extent responsible for this ecstasy.

Orgasm Contested

In the late 1991, Orgasmologists attended the first International Conference on Orgasm in New Delhi where quite a few sexual myths were dispelled. Indian women do not have as much orgasm as their counter parts in America and other Western Countries. There are several reasons for that. Basically due to the fact that the Indian Society is a men-dominated society and they think that women are merely play things and they are meant to give sexual pleasure rather than enjoy the sexual act. Unhappy wives make for unhappy partners. If men wanted more responsive wives, they should treat them as equals and seek a more loving and trustful relationship. The Federation of Feminist Health Centres in the U.S. listed as many as 19 separate parts of the female body which included in all contagious structures, that directly contributed to orgasm. Rebecca Chalkar said at the conference, that women should know that their sexual anatomy is in no way inferior to that of men's and functions in the same way as men. When Dr. Alica K. Ladas from New York stressed that the male and the female genitals are both unified continuous organs and in the case of women it even extends into the rectal area too, that the clitoris in women plays similar part as the penis in men, of which many are ignorant about. Dr. L. Mohadikar stressed that lack of knowledge about the techniques is the major drawback in achieving orgasm in mating. She stressed that love play should be extended over a longer time and the 'Love Touch' technique of the partners during the day accumulates sexual tension and helps in releasing orgasm when fuelled. She as well told us that the couple should try for a more trustful and equitable relationship in their day-to-day activities in order to achieve orgasmic pleasures. The partners should have total acceptance having mental and physical freedom to enjoy sexual pleasures. N. Jankiramiah, a professor of Psychiatry at the National Institute of Mental Health and Neurosciences, in Bangalore was of the opinion that in many cases, it is seen that the neurotic depression of the Indian women was due to their inferiority complex for the success and achievements in their jobs or due to inheritance of property, or change in the power of structure with their husbands.

Hence, in order that both men and women should enjoy social and sexual happiness, the status of women should be uplifted in the society.

Viropause Syndrome in Men

It is generally felt, that because of the menopause of the females, their orgasm and enthusiasm for work, and zest for life, is only short lived, and that male members are much better off that way. They can enjoy sexual life and orgasm for longer length of time. But there is some controversy about it.

Dr. Malcolm Carruthers, Director of the Hormonal Health Centre, in Harley Street, for 10 years, believes that men have probably always suffered from serious middle life crisis, but they did not like to admit that. Like "Menopause" in Women, Dr. Carruthers calls it as "Viropause", in men, heading for tapering of their sex drive and impending impotence. At the start it becomes irritable, associated with depression and tiredness. Aches and night sweats start from the age of 40 onwards. This, Dr. Carruthers opines, is due to the failure of the body's own *Testoterone* to race around, as it once did in mid thirties. Dr. Carruthers says that if controlled amounts of *Testoterone* is administered into the body, then it can restore the Energy, Libido and Confidence. But again Dr. Gordon Williams, an Urologist at Hammer Smith Hospital, has expressed fear that long term *Testoterone* treatment could lead to *Prostate Tumors*. Dr. Carruthers asserts that, when female Hormone Replacement Treatment (HRT) was started about 20 years back, women faced such similar drawbacks due to ignorance only. But if the male HRT is done under monitoring, then the amount of *Testoterone* administration is controlled, and after a few months *Testoterone* pellets are implanted in the buttock while his reactions are being monitored.

Recently Barnard Collen of West London who is 47 years old had been under TRT for three and a half years. He feels that his irritability has decreased considerably and his general libido has been enhanced.

What I try to impress upon you is that whether you are agreeable to undergo HRT treatments or not, the fact remains that between the age of 40 and 50 years, men's Libido start decreasing, as the Libido of women drops during and after the menopause.

Again if you refer to the diagram of the brain and the notes regarding Pituitary, Thalamus and Hypothalamus Glands given at the beginning of this chapter, you will realise that these glands, in conjugation with the Cerebrum and the Cerebral Cortex gives the orgasm that we get. But to pinpoint the regions which are responsible for the amazing orgasm, extensive research is essential. This, we shall be able to solve in near future. As a matter of fact, all the five senses that we have, contribute to reach the stage of ecstasy. The sight, the hearing, the smell, the taste and the skin sensation, all congregate to create the euphoria of feelings of the state of ecstasy, the orgasm.

The Sex Education

Sexology is a specialised subject. The anatomy of sex and the functions of the organs of the homosapines are taught in medical schools. Though this is a specialised subject, monopolised by medical profession only, nevertheless, the common man has got every right to know its basic principles. In order to know the basic principles, he has to have some preliminary knowledge of the sex organs and their functions.

The lack of knowledge of the sex organs and their functions, leads the young boys and girls, to misuse the sex functions and sometimes they become perverted also. Having realised its seriousness, the academic institutions abroad and also India, they have started taking special classes with charts, slides and audio-visuals to educate the students about this science. This education,guards against the pitfalls in this game of sex. In the absence of sex education, men and women, and specially the young boys and girls will have no taboo and will indulge indiscriminately in the act of sex and will be promiscuous.

As it was told earlier the male spermatozoa is responsible for fertilizing the ova or the egg from the female. This spermatozoa or sperm, as it is termed in short, is produced in the testicles of the male. In the human being, the sperms are manufactured right from the age of 10. From the diagram it will be revealed where from these sperms are manufactured and vehicled down to the male sex organ (external).

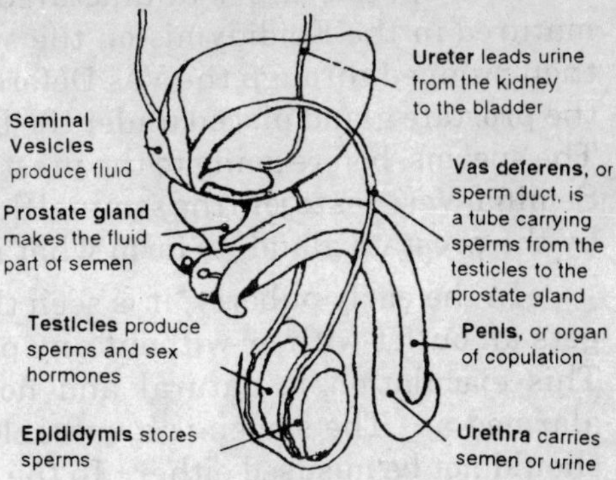

Fig. 9 : The Male Sex Organ

The gonads, or sex glands, are the testes, or testacles in men. The two testes in men are stimulated by the pituitary gland which control their activity by means of Gonadotrophin Hormones. These Hormones have got two functions:

(a) to manufacture sperm cells, used for giving new life (producing babies)

(b) To affect the growth and well being of the whole body (by the Sex Hormone - Testosterone).

These Hormones start acting on the growing man from the age of 10, at puberty, but they are more profound from the age of 12 to 14 only, when the changes in the shape of the body and voice, look and character is more perceptible. In an accident or otherwise, if the testicles have to be removed (castration) then the secondary sexual characteristics are only changed.

We were discussing about how the male spermatozoa is responsible for creating another life (by fertilizing the female egg cell). But if the same spermatozoa is stopped in the onward journey, then it can help in curbing excessive growth of human population also. This is done by Vasectomy, the process of severing the sperm duct, either by cutting the Vas Deferens (the sperm duct) or tieing it up. There are various other methods also for contraception, both for the male and the female which are not discussed here.

The sperms are manufactured in the tubules and are matured in the Epididymis on the sides of the testes, and are then pumped through the Vas Deferens (or the Sperm Duct) to the prostate gland placed under the bladder (for storing urine). The sperms, before going to the prostate gland, passes on to the Seminal Vesicles to join the seminal fluid, which is manufactured by the prostate gland, to form what is called the Semen.

In the early puberty, it is seen that sometimes this semen gets an outlet with or without any provocation or excitement. This ejaculation is natural and normal and should not be alarmed at. The semen is a valuable asset of the male and it should not be misused either. In the youth, it should be frozen in the bank, as if. Then only at a later stage of life, we can enjoy a better life.

Millions of sperms are manufactured in the coiled tubules inside the testicles everyday from as early as 10 to 14 years of age upto a very late stage in life in the male.

The Female Sex Organ

In the animals, as in plants, it is necessary for the male sperms to reach the egg cells from the female, to give birth to a new one. As we are concentrating on human beings only, let us study where to find the eggs and how and where they meet the sperm cell. The Diagram below shows the female organ.

For the common man, it is the vagina of the female body which is the prime part that is responsible for giving birth to a baby. But actually, it is only the gateway for the citadel, known as the womb (uterus), where all the ceremony of holding the baby is performed. But, between the vagina and the womb, there lies the Cervix, which protects the womb from entering of any infection or any foreign body, by a mucus plug, except for a few days in the menstrual cycle of a woman.

Normally, the long road to the conception actually begins about seven months before a girl child is born (approximately after two months of pregnancy of her mother), when microscopic eggs begin to form in the buds of the new conception, that will ultimately become the ovary of the matured woman, later.

The woman is born with about 2 million eggs, but by puberty the normal degeneration reduces the number to about

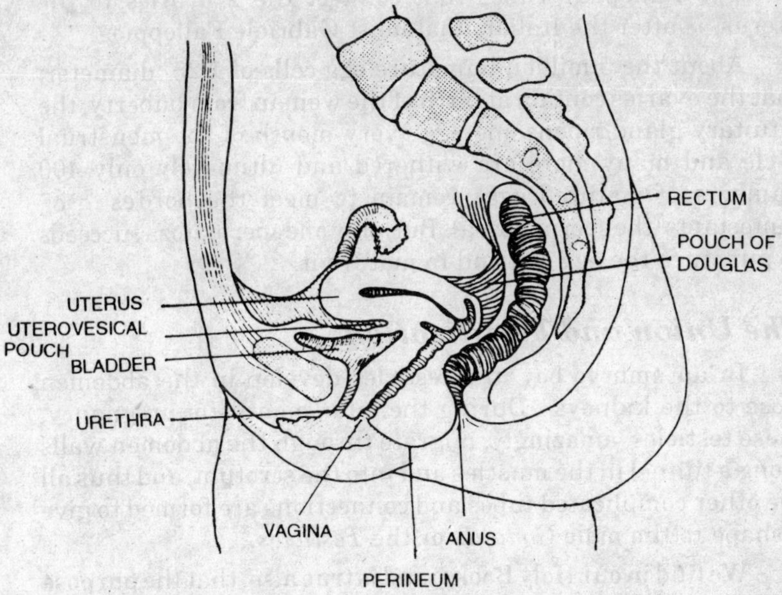

Fig. 10 : The Female Sex Organ

400,000 (four lacs). Starting from puberty of the woman, thousands of egg cells either wither away or disappear and ultimately the number of egg cells she can effectively use is approximately 400 only.

Whereas a man churns out the sperms at the rate of 1000 of second or (30 billions a year), a woman never produces any new egg. Ultimately, when woman exhausts to supply the egg cells, her ovary will virtually shut down and this event is termed as menopause. Recent studies show that it is the age of the eggs and not the age of the reproductive system that causes fertility, which decline after the age of 40 in general. The initial limited supply of eggs, is perhaps the chief reason that fertility of a woman decreases sharply with the age.

The poet had rightly said, "Fraility, thy name is the woman". How delicate and weak is the woman!!

In a matured woman, the egg cells are manufactured in the ovaries (two of them on either side of the utreus). In a normal (menstrual) cycle only one egg, alternately from each ovary, will be released to the Fallopian Tube for possible fertilisation.

The Fallopian Tubes that connect the 2 ovaries to the uterus, is after the Italian anatomist Gabriele Falloppio.

About the 5 million immature egg cells of 1/25" diameter, that the ovaries contain at birth of the woman from puberty, the pituitary gland ripens one egg every month of the menstrual cycle and many more are withered and ultimately only 400 numbers of matured eggs remain to meet the hordes of contestants (the spermatozoa). But, only one spermatoza succeeds to puncture the egg cell and to mature it.

The Union and Fertilization

In an embryo boy, the testicles develop in the abdomen close to the kidneys. During the later months of pregnancy, these testicles, amazingly, migrate through the abdomen walls along a tunnel in the muscles and into the scrotum, and thus all the other complicated tubes and connections are formed to give a shape to the male *Gonalds* or the *Testicles*.

We find in our Holy Books, and is true also, that the purpose of the sexual intercourse is to create a new human life only. This sexual intercourse is generally preceded by conscious sexual excitement in both the male and the female partners. When excited, the empty spaces around the Clitoris and the Labia Minora is moistened to prepare the valva to receive the male organ for the holy ceremony.

The nature of man is that he gets aroused quicker than the woman and that lasts for a shorter period only than that of the woman. Hence, mutual adjustments are very necessary to have orgasm for a longer period together. At the height of excitement when orgasm is experienced, semen is forced out of the urethra and intermittent ejaculation occurs.

A healthy man generates about 1000 sperms per second and at every union about 500 million sperms are released into the vagina. But usually as the cervix is sealed by the mucus plug all the time, the sperms do not get access to the uterus unless the mouth of the cervix is opened for a very short period in the menstrual period of women. The average monthly cycle lasts for about 28 days, since the age of 12 to 14 years of the girl till she is 50 years old, or sometime earlier or later.

Usually from the 28th day after the menstrual cycle, starts the unfertilised egg and the lining of the womb are discarded in the menstrual flow which lasts till the 4th day of the new cycle of the next menstrual cycle. At that time only in one of the ovaries, the follicles start growing by the aid of the pituitary gland which lies at the base of the brain.

From the 12th day after the new menstrual period starts, one of the folicles produces the Hormone Oestrogen which helps to build up the lining of the womb, preparing it to receive a fertilised egg and the womb is also filled with a fluid.

After the 14th day, the pituitary gland produces the Hormone LH, and thus one egg is released from one of the ovaries and picked up by the fringes of the Fallopian Tube (FT). If the egg is not fertilised (by the spermatoza) during its passage through the FT, the egg dies within 48 hrs.

We see from this, that it is the period from 12th to the 14th day after the menstrual cycle starts, the pregnancy is expected to happen. Hence the period from 5th to 11th and from 17th to 27th day of the menstrual cycle may be termed as the Safe Periods, when the chances of pregnancy are minimum. But strictly speaking, the period between 16th and 20th day is not very safe either.

Thus, when the spermatozoa are received in the womb, electrical messages are sent through the *Fallopian Tubes* to the released egg cell. Then the innumerable sperm cells start their journey from the womb to the single egg cell in the *Fallopian Tubes*. Only when these sperms receive chemical signals from their would be bride (the egg cell). Like the Indian Swayamvar Ceremony, where from a number of contestants only one is chosen, the tadpole like sperm cells try to penetrate the single egg cell, but alas, one and only one sperms cell can puncture the hard barrier of the egg cell by its own Enzymes. Other sperms, thus defeated, retreat and are destroyed within a few hours only.

After the egg is fertilised in the upper part of the *Fallopian Tube* (FT), it starts travelling down the FT into the womb (the uterus). Pregnancy occurs only if the egg cell is fertilised within

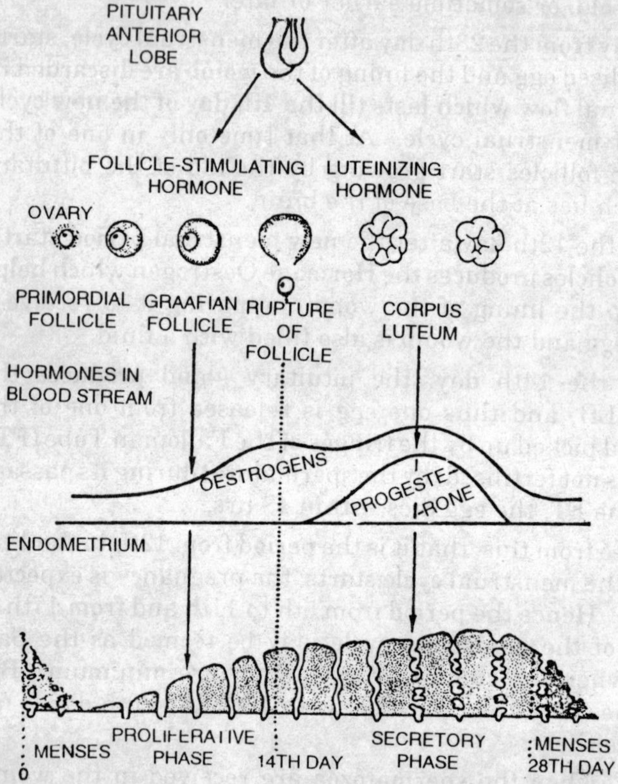

Fig. 11 : The Menstrual Cycle

6 to 12 Hrs. of leaving the ovary. A disc shaped structure called the Placenta, develops in the womb during the pregnancy and is attached to it generally at the upper part of the same. The other end of the Placenta is connected to the Umbilical Cord, through which the foetus (the developing baby) obtain nourishment and oxygen. The discharges and the waste products are passed on through the mother's body for disposal. In an abnormal condition, the fertilized egg cell is attached at the lower end of the womb, which is called the Placenta Praevia. At this, there are chances of the Placenta being detached during birth of the baby or even earlier, resulting in abortion.

The story of the birth of a child is not so easy as is described here briefly. More details will be out of the scope of this book, and the common man will not be interested in it either.

The Unusual Pregnancy

Whatever have been told above are for normal fertility in the human sexual reproduction. But infertility may affect millions of couples, rich and poor, all over the world. In the process of investigating the causes and cures of infertility, the doctors have learnt, more and more of the complicated mechanism of conception. Doctors, today can manipulate virtually every aspect of the reproductive cycle—from artificially ripening the eggs in the ovary to, inserting individual sperm directly into the egg's inner membrane.

Sometime in 1979, two British doctors, Patrick Steptoe and Robert Edwards, engineered the birth of "Louise Brown", the first 'Test Tube Baby' by *In-Vitro-Firtilization* (IVF). Thereafter, this technology has been exported to France, Australia, U.S.A. and other countries also. As the technology advances, more and more families are placed together with the borrowed eggs and borrowed wombs.

Borrowed Eggs and Borrowed Wombs

But, it is seen that even under best circumstances,—a fertile couple having united at the optimum period in the woman's menstrual cycle *i.e.,* between the 12th and 14th day after start of the 'period' as it is usually called, the pregnancy may not mature, 3 times out of 4, if the woman is over 35, when the egg cells are scanty or when the sperms are defective or in short supply or for many other reasons.

However, after the egg is fertilised, the hormones from the females, play an active part to continue the process of pregnancy. In case, the body hormones of the pregnant mother, are not sufficient or efficient enough then the Estrogen and Progesterone Hormones are administered in the female body, which supplement the natural supply of these. But many a times, it is seen that these may create havoc also. In case of complicated conditions, IVF (In-Verto-Fertilization), ZIFT (Zygote-Intra-

Fallopian-Transfer) or GIFT (Gamate-Intra-Fallopian-Transfer) techniques are adopted to solve the problems

You will be interested to know some of the special processes involved in the insemination and fertilisation processes, as described below:

(a) Artificial insemination is a process in which the doctor deposits the semen from the husband of the female or from a donor male directly or from the semen bank, into the egg's inner membrane through the vagina.

(b) *In-Virto* (In Glass) fertilisation is a process in which the doctor combines the sperm with the egg in a petri-dish, outside the body and then transfers the same into the womb.

(c) *Gift* is the process which is a variation in the *In-vitro* method in which the sperm and the unfertilised egg are inserted directly into the fallopian Tube.

(d) *Zift* is the process in which the eggs and the sperms are mixed in a 'Patri Dish' and the resulting pre-embryos are then placed in the Fallopian Tube.

Several methods have been devised to give the sperms a boost, including 'Microinjection', wherein the sperm is inserted directly into the egg by means of a microscopic needle by making a tiny hole in the egg's protective shell.

In April 1991, scientists from Israel and United States of America, reported a new finding, to help the Infertilised couples. They found that the sperms respond only to those eggs that emit "come hether" signal to the sperms and not to all. This indicated that "attraction may indeed be a key process in fertilization", which is opined recently by Israel Scientist Michael Eisenbach. Also the scientists in South Korea are experimenting the freezing and storing of unfertilized eggs, sperms and also embryos (fertilised eggs).

Eventually it will not be out of place here to mention that the first test tube baby (common name for the birth of a baby by artificial insemination), born in India sometime in 1988, was by the help of Dr. Indira Hinduja and Dr. T.C. Anand in Bombay.

Again Dr. Geeta Pandya, claims that she started the first sperm Bank in Jaslok Hospital in Bombay in 1974. Notwithstanding the increasing demand for test tube babies, there are only three or four sperm banks in Bombay. And that, in all of North India, only Sir Ganga Ram Hospital, in Delhi has facilities for production of test tube babies.

The major reason for the lack of sperm banks, is the requirement of maintenance of temperature as low as (-196°C) to ensure safe storing of the sperms. This can be achieved only by arranging the constant supply of liquid Nitrogen for this purpose.

Dr. M. Kochar, who has set up the Invertro-Fertilization Centre in 1991, found that when the ova and sperm are placed in the petri-dish for fertilisation, the Y chromosome (the male factor of the sperm) which has a higher mortality than the X chromosome (the female factor of the sperm) "reaches the ova faster" than the X factor. Hence in the fertilization that takes place generally a male embryo is formed. In short, he claims that in the Inverto Fertilizaion Technique the higher conception of males is due to the faster fertilizaion process of the Y sperms. Whereas, in Britain, government intervened and ensured that not more than three fertilized embryos could be transplanted in the womb from the 'Petri', so that even all the three mature, the mother does not have more than triplets, but in India there is no such restrictions here as yet.

Generally it is seen that unlike animals, human beings give birth to one baby at a time. But multiple pregnancies can also occur in several ways which is discussed below:

(1) When the ovaries have been stimulated artificially or otherwise by hormone, two eggs may be released and fertilized at the same time. The result is called Faternal Twins (non-identical twins).

(2) When by any reason, a single fertilized egg immediately divides into two, and each cell become implanted separately on to the womb, a twin may develop of the same sex and even may have the same hair colour also.

(3) Again, if the correct hormonal changes don't take place and ovulation does not stop immediately after the start of pregnancy (which is normally the case), then a second egg may be released and be fertilised so that two babies develop in the womb one later than the first, probably after a month.

(4) Triplets, quards (fours) and quins (fives) usually result from a combination of more than one egg and also by the division of a fertilised egg. In these cases some babies are identical and other are not.

Generally women do not conceive after the menopause. But, recently Dr. Mark Sauer at the University of Southern California has been successful in making a woman of 52, pregnant who had menopause years earlier. He took an egg from a young woman and artificially inseminated with sperm from the husband of the old lady and the menopause syndrome was thus defeated.

Failures in Conception

If the man and the woman are healthy and devoid of mental tension, they are successful in the efforts of conception and the woman gives birth to a baby after 280 days from the Ist day of menstruation prior to the union (this calculation holds if the female menstruates at regular interval of 28 days). They should unite in the period from the 12th to 14th day of menstrual cycle from the Ist day, after menstruation. Generally, it is seen that three out of four trials are failures. There are various reasons for it:

(1) The semen from the male may contain very "small number" of healthy sperm cells in a single ejaculation which may not make way to the Fallopian Tube (F.T.). This *Infertility* may also be due to sluggishness or imperfection (unvigorous) of sperm cells.

(2) On the part of the woman, if the 'periods' are irregular or the ovulation do not occur, or there is some defect or disease in the Fallopian Tube or in the lining of the womb, then also there is no conception. These defects may be rectified by proper 'hormone' or other treatments.

(3) For men, 'Impotence' may be a very common type of defect wherein they cannot perform the actual process or do not reach orgasm so as to effect ejaculation to implant sperms. This defect can be treated by physical as well as psychological methods.

(4) "Frigidity" in a woman is mostly due to psychological reasons, but disorder of the sex organs cannot be ruled out either.

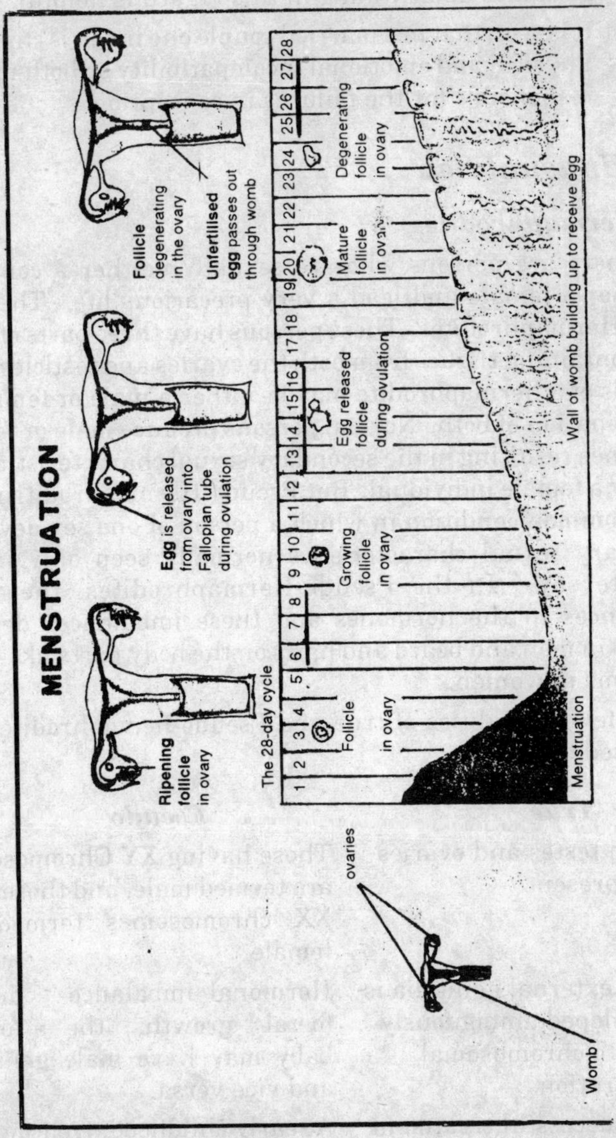

Fig. 12 : The Menstrual Cycle

(5) Conception does not usually occur if the couple do the act, in improper methods due to their ignorance. Proper guidance and training in this regard is helpful.

(6) It is seen that in a married couple one in ten is childless. Physical and emotional incompatibility or both may be responsible for the failures in conception.

The Unusual Sex

(a) Hermaphrodites

There are persons who are sexually neither a complete male nor a female and lead a very precarious life. They are called Hermaphrodites. These persons have three parts of their body containing tissues from both the ovaries and testicles. The genitals of a hermaphrodite may be either a male or female or a combination of both. Normal persons produce male or female hormones resulting in the secondary sexual characteristics of a male or a female individual. But Pseudo-Hermaphroditism is a more common condition in which a person of one sex develops secondary sexual characteristics normally seen only in the opposite sex. In the Pseudo-Hermaphrodites, there are imbalances in the hormones and these imbalances develop breasts in men and beard and hairs on the body parts like chest and arms in women.

A few specialities of true and Pseudo-hemaphrodites are tabulated below:

	True	*Pseudo*
1.	Both testes and ovaries are present.	Those having XY Chromosomes are termed male, and those with XX chromosomes termed as female.
2.	The external genitalia is developed ambiguously due to chromosomal aberration.	Hormonal imbalance during foetal growth, the female baby may have male genitalia and vice versa.
3.	No successful treatment has yet been achieved.	At early childhood, treatment is possible for rectification and cure.

From the old literatures we find that people were aware of the third sex as early as in 425 B.C. Herodotus (525-484 B.C.) mentions about the Enarees - women like soothsayers. Plato (427-347 B.C.) wrote in his 'Symposium', that human beings were of three types—"Man, women and a Union of the two". Again Ovid (43 B.C.-17 A.D.) relates a story that young Hermaphroditus (also called Aphrodite), son of Mercury, met the nymph Salamacis. She also fell in love and ran after him. She, twining herself around him prayed to God, so that God does not separate herself from him ever. The limbs, thus melted in clinging embrace and a single from possessed of two natures, neither male nor female, but both and neither.

For these Pseudo-Hermaphrodites, the scientists are trying their hands to rectify the disorders by hormone treatments and plastic surgery. But for the Hermaphrodites nothing much has been achieved to change the sex. Socially and economically they are very much unprevileged. If they are given facilities for rehabilitation, they can lead a normal and better social life. They really deserve sympathy, care and guidance from the society. If they are educated, and trained, they can as well be fitted in various branches of the society, which surely will uplift their own 'status' as well as the condition of the society.

(*b*) *Homo Sexuals*

"Homosexuality" is love for some one of the same sex; it may be between two men or two women. The latter couple is termed as Lesbian. Again, 'Bisexuals', may have sexual relationships with members of both the sexes.

Some theorists say that Homosexuality results due to hormonal imbalance. Other psychoanalysts opine that Homosexuality has an emotional and psychological foundation.

It has been told earlier in this book that upto a certain age, the boys and girls have their love partners of the same sex and at a later stage, they choose their mate from the opposite sex. This is normal. But if this Homosexual attitude persists and if they are not corrected before entering into adulthood they become an absolute menace to the society. They turn into true Homo-sexuals. There are male and female types in lesbians as well, which is prevalent in male Homo-sexuals also. Homo-sexuals as well as the lesbians generally live together as devoted married couples.

Scientists have not yet been successful in curing the Homosexual attitude by hormonal treatments.

(c) *Oedipus, Electra and Orestes Complex*

'Oedipus' complex or 'Edipus' Complex', is defined as the child's repressed desire for sexual intercourse with the parent of the opposite sex. Strictly speaking, Oedipus Complex is referred to for boys and the Electra Complex is referred to the corresponding desire of the girl child. In the Greek Tragedy, Sophocles wrote that the hero Oedipus unwittingly killed his father and married his mother. In his youth the hero had his feet pierced (hence swollen = Oedipus in Greek) and he was left to die, but was saved later by a shepherd boy and he thus was able to fulfil his desires.

Dr. Freud relates that in the early childhood upto the puberty, knowing the child's desires, the parents try to suppress the urge of the child. As the libido continues to demand an outlet, the child obtains vicarious satisfaction in the sexual relations with the parent of the desired one. As a matter of fact the Oedipus stage of development is the early childhood is the manifestation of the early Genital Phase of Development.

Sex Perversions

It was discussed in the earlier chapters that if the 'Love' element is not cherished and groomed properly, the 'Hate' and 'Sex' elements make a headway, and it devours our psyche. In other words, "Thanatos" prevails in our character and the Hate element in amalgamation with the Sex element in us, plays havoc. The result is a perverted personality. A few perversions of Thanatos are listed below:

01. Child Molestation
02. Eveteasing.
03. Rape.
04. Gang Violence.
05. Gang Rape.
06. Murder.
07. Suicide
08. Abortion
09. Oral Sadism.
10. Sadism.
11. Masochism.
12. Exhibitionism.
13. Voyeusm.
14. Live Togetherism

On 30.11.1992, a report was published in the daily Newspaper which was compiled by the National Crime Records Bureau and was discussed in a meeting attended by the Prime Minister and several other important members of the Parliament in India. It said that in India,

(a) A rape is committed every 54 minutes,

(b) A molestation every 26 minutes.

(c) An abduction every 43 minuets.

(d) Eve Teasing every 54 Minutes

(e) Dowry death every 102 minutes,

(f) Criminal offence against women every 7 minutes.

These figures show our moral degradation and our perverted nature due to not properly nourishing the love elements in us. There are various reasons for these perversions as to why these are increasing in our society.

In another report from Washington, published on the 28th July, 1992, relates how the juveniles, some as young as six years old are identified as sex offenders. Again close to 30 per cent of the people arrested on all rape charges in 1990 there, were under 21 years of age. For all other sex offences including exhibitionism, voyeurism, fondling etc., 16 per cent of those arrested were under 18 years of age.

On 28.07.1992, another report was published in the City of Buffalo, N.Y., about 20 women that marched across the Peace Bridge, baring their breasts in the public, who all won the court battle for policies barring woman, for baring their breasts.

Another event in Bangalore, India, was reported on the 02.03.1992, that a 27 years old man reportedly had sex with 26 women, before strangulating them, during a period of only 3 years. This story reveals that the 27 years old stone cutter, had a pent up 'Mortido' in him and he had some saddist element in him, which induced him to achieve orgasm in the act of sex in this adventurous way, and ultimately the Mortido in him induced him to kill (destroy) this subjects and have ecstasy. As was told earlier in this book, most of the crimes are committed during the period of 18 to 28 years, and here also the concerned person's period of activity was from 24 to 27 years only.

Perversions Classifications

Sexual perversions are socially unacceptable form of the sexual conduct point of view of which the most common types are, Fetishism, Exhibitionism, Sadism and Masochism.

Fetchism is a perversion wherein an inaminate object is believed to have magical powers for sexual arousal; those may be stockings, handkerchief, lingerie (women's underwear and night clothes) or the symbol of phallus or animate body of non-sexual cadre like, hair, feet etc.

In Exhibitionism, the person achieves pleasure by the display of his or her body parts.

Whereas in Voyeurism the person obtains sexual gratification by watching others undress or engaged in sexual activities.

Much has been told earlier regarding Sadism and Masochism, but some more are added below:

Child Molestation, Eve Teasing, Rape etc. are nothing but perverted sex, while 'Gang Violence', 'Murder', 'Suicide' and 'Abortion' are the activities of Thanatos, the controller of the hate element in us. *Exhibitionism* is again a sex perversion from which the exhibitor is amused by showing his body and gets enormous pleasure out of it.

Oral Sadism is the desire to hurt or destroy by biting or chewing. The infant gets satisfaction from nursing, biting and chewing. This is the infant stage of sex satisfaction. If the child is not stopped or persuaded to refrain from these activities in this 'Passive Stage', he then at a later stage, becomes actively aggressive. If the sucking is unnecessarily prolonged at the infant stage, he becomes, overoptimistic as well as dependent at a later stage of life. If the oral activities are over-encouraged (as some children are allowed to suck the breast or an artificial nipple for several more years) then at a later stage, he may become talkative, or munching masters or a voracious eater or a chain smoker.

To add to the list of sex perversions, there is yet another type of sex manipulation, basically common among people in the western countries. But of late, it is seen that Indians are also following suit. This is termed as 'Live Together'. In this, men and women live together like married couple without going into the formalities of a regular marriage. In the western countries, the society as well as the Court accepts 'living together'. So much so, that their offsprings, if any, due to this live together, are also legalised in many parts of the western countries.

We had learnt that "Marriages are made in Heaven" and also that "Marriage is a sacred and religious aspect."

The argument of those who augment "Live Together", is that they cannot decry "Live Together", considering this as a legal prostitution; because marriage is also nothing but another legal prostitution. If the 'Live Together' is fully legalised throughout the world, then there remains no bar classifying any union of male and female, as prostitution. But this cannot be so.

In our Indian holy books, we learnt that "Puthrthey Kryatey Verja," meaning that "Take a wife to have a son (boy)." According to this theory, to have sex outside marriage is nothing but prostitution.

Hence, those persons who advocate "Live Together" do not cajole sympathy but only evokes pity. God will never pardon them for this type of perversion.

This craving for having sex outside marriage is due to the defused Libido in us. This cannot be evaded fully, but can very well be kept under control.

Supremacy of Women Over Men

Though superficially, we see that females are passive sexual partners only, but studies conducted by *Small*, *Russel*, *Baker* and *Bellis*, reveal that females have extraordinary biological skill to ensure that only the sperm from the favoured partner is allowed to fertilize the egg.

Charles Darwin postulated, in his book, 'The Descent of Men and Selection in Relation of Sex', in 1871, that a dominant male will choose the female and hence decide the genetic destiny of their race. He also discussed in it, as to why females and males look and behave differently.

But Meredith F. Small, tracing the evolution of human female behaviour, and re-examining the faminist revolution conduced in 1970, by the scientists, opines that females are not passive spectators only. They are sexually assertive and eager for novelty and variety.

Another biologist Rebert Jay Russel, in his recently published book, "Evolution of Power in Sex and Love", revealed that human females, like those of Lemurs, prefer mating with males that are strong, confident, high ranking and preferably romantic. As the behaviour of Lemurs are similar to that of the human species, we have reasons to believe it as correct.

The statement of Russel is supported by the painstaking evidences gathered by the two Manchester University Researchers, Robbin Baker and Mark Bellis, published in the "Animal Bhehaviour", which reveal that the females of animals, lower in the evolutionary ladder have developed extraordinary skills in ensuring that only the sperm of the favoured partner is retained in case of multiple copulations with so many males, which is very common in the animals. To establish this fact for human beings, statistics were collected and it was revealed that out of 3000 copulations as many as 76 were declared as double mating. By genetic studies in the humans, it is widely believed that about 10 per cent of the children in certain samples studied, have been fathered by someone other than the officially declared parent. From this, it is deducted that during the positive period of the menstrual cycle, if there is a second mating from a different partner within five days of the first copulation, then the battle starts, and who wins, fertilizes the egg. This is possible because, only less than about one per cent of the 500 and odd millions of sperms ejaculated, are egg-getter sperms, specialised for fertilization. The remainder only serve to block the rival sperms from joining the egg. Baker and Bellis are of the opinion that human females, prefer a set of genes of their choice, which practice is not very different from that of the lower animals.

From this, it is evident that the female egg definitely dictates, which sperm is to be accepted and which not, for effective fertilization. The sperms in this case are only silent spectators.

Hence, the female eggs definitely have a better say than the male sperms. And similarly, we have seen that females have the first and last say over men in our day-to-day life also.

5
LOOKING BEYOND

We have thus known the various stages of sex and the sexual aberrations. We have also learnt that sex is not a crime, and cannot be discarded altogether, even we try to, because, it is part of us, and is also an inherent one.

We have also seen in the previous chapters, how love spreads its wings over all the good as well as the evil aspects of the universe. We have seen, how and how much, this love can be our messiah and is able to protect us from the catastrophes and save us from the ensuing disasters.

We have also seen, how Lovė has an edge on sex. It is true that sex is prone to develop and cherish in Love. But, this also cannot be defined that sex has got its own entity. The male sex has its own dimensions and a fragrance, as the female similarly has its own, but the hue is different. Both these two sexes have to exist simultaneously. Because one is inevitable for the other.

But this co-existence is also a tough job. Both the male and female sex have got their own identities and hence they are different. Hence the co-existence becomes extremely difficult, unless there is a feeling of live and let live attitude. For them to co-exist, the male and the female have to share their pleasures and sorrows, as it is a must.

This male and the female sex are different in all aspects. They are different physically, biologically, hormonally, socially, temperamentally, intellectually, psychologically and in various other aspects. One of them, is extrovert and the other is introvert; one is tough and the other is soft and amicable. The male in general, tries to ride over the female and the female, by nature, is submissive. For this reason, the female sometimes opens up and retaliates also.

For this anomaly there is an eternal in fight among the two sexes. We can call it as the battle of the sexes. This combat, between the two sexes can be eased, if there is an understanding between them. And this can only be achieved and the patch up is possible only by the tool called love.

We have also seen in the last chapter that the females have got a number of handicaps, sexually as well as physically. Sexual handicaps are discussed in details much earlier. As regards the physical drawbacks, some are very evident. Their muscles are weaker and limbs are shorter, their lower torso is disproportinately heavy, the dimensions of the feet are shorter etc. These shortcomings are compensated to a great extent by the nature. As they are the creation of the same God that created men, they deserve equanamity in dealings and treatments. They should never be pitied and looked down as inferiors. The female sex is linked and bonded to the male sex from the eternity. They are inseparable so as to transform the world into a paradise.

The Downfall and Uplift of Female

All these days, there is a hue and cry for the imminent need for the Indian women, as if there is an impending danger hovering over their heads. We otherwise, will not be able to save our society from a grave catastrophy.

Why, at all, it has become necessary, even to think for any need to uplift women? Have they really been drifted down as low as that? If at all, you think, that it is so, then who all are responsible for this downfall? Is it not the male dominated society which is at fault for this downfall? A glance at the past Indian History will throw some light on this aspect.

In the very early years of Indian history we find that the vedic rights and the then environment, placed the women at a level much above the men folks. The women used to be the pioneer for all the celebrations and functions; and in short, this situation was, in all the walks of the society. They were at the helm only. But at that time as there were no force acting, to sustain the status of Hindu women of India, the then women lost ground to challenge men. But now, in the present society the majority of women are the cause of their self destruction. From our old religious scriptures we find that during the Vedic Period (2500 B.C. to 1500 B.C.) women had a respectable status which was comparable to that of men. And at times, the respect enjoyed by women excelled that of men.

According to A.S. Altelkar, "In the vedic period the sacred

thread (Upanayan) was very common for the girls and they had to undergo a regular course of education like 'Theology' and 'Philosophy' and a considerable number of women had also to adopt the teaching carrier". From this, it is revealed that the women of that period attained such a level of education that enabled them to perform the religious rites correctly and also they were able to take up profession of teaching as a carrier. Women of that period enjoyed a status at home as well as in the society, equal to that of men. In those times certain religious functions could not be performed without the aid of women. This would shock our present society!

Polygamy was not permitted at that time, but nevertheless widow re-marriage was allowed. This period, previous to 1500 B.C., was called "the Golden period of women".

In the next period, *i.e.,* from 1500 B.C. to 500 B.C., taboos to women's freedom cropped in. During this period, women who used to go to the centres for learning, were discouraged and dissociated for going out of home; and only the family members like father, brother and other male relatives could teach. Men started sharing the responsibility of performing the religious functions after they had studied the 'Vedas' (Indian religious scriptures).

According to Altelkar, the women, in this period, still enjoyed the privileges over men, and they used to perform the religious functions, in the absence of the male members, when they used to go out for operations like conquest and consideration. The women of those days, thus started taking active part in agriculture and in the manufacturing cloth, and weapons like bows, arrows etc. Of course, they were useful members of the society, but the status was not so high as that of men.

Thereafter, came a period of drastic downfall of women, in our "Indian Society". This was between 500 B.C. and 500 A.D. Aryan males (Indian Hindus) had good means of overriding on women by marrying the indigenous (native) population. As these Non-Aryan Hindu women, had no knowledge of Sanskrit (an ancient Indian language), they were not able to partake in religious activities. This was also not allowed by their male members. Thus, gradually, women were discouraged and debarred from taking active part in Vedic and other sacred activities, ultimately causing the lowering of their status.

During this period another new factor cropped up. It was proclaimed that only a son and not a daughter could perform certain religious functions and rites. This naturally, necessitated in the procreation of a son. Thus, with the passing of time, 'Man' became superior to 'Women' in all religious as well as social activities.

Then immediately afterwards, followed the 'Buddhist Period'. In the then society, they again uplifted the women and gave them a place of honour by cherishing religious training to them. But this formula did not survive for long.

In the post-Buddhist period, there was a conflict of religious and social thoughts. In this humdrum, the status of women was at stake. The practice of women re-marriage went into oblivion, and thus the right of women to inherit property was not accepted, but all the same they were entitled to a maintenance.

At this juncture, Manu the law maker, proclaimed, that a maiden should be protected by her father, a wife by her husband and a widow by her sons. Thus they were considered unfit for freedom and deserved no independence, and thus they were kept under the authority of the male, at all the stages of their life. At this juncture, it was necessary for the women to try their uplift, themselves. But unfortunately they did not try their hand at that. As a result there was a further downfall of women during this period.

During the next period, that is from 500 A.D. to 1200 A.D., Hindu religion had become complicated. The women being least educated among the people and that too having only a few rights and privileges, they blindly followed the dictums and rules laid down by the exponents of Puranic Literature. They did not attempt to exercise their individual judgements and had not fought for their lost status and position on the society.

From the fag end of the Buddhist period, the downfall of women started. And after the Muslim invasion and the British rule, things became worse. The Indian women were taken as commodities, to be possessed and ruled over only. Then at the advent of the Western culture in our society, our women folk, being less educated, could not understand the bright side of the Western culture. They only tried to adopt the means to achieve instant pleasure, superficial glamour and pomp. This was a prime hindrance to their progress.

Then when the National Movement started for ousting the Britishers, a handful of women tried to achieve their legitimate demand. This effort for uplifting, was not for their personal end, but it was for National Cause. After the Independence was achieved in India, women realised their true worth. They then fought for their education and grooming. But lot more is now left undone. If the urge for cheap pleasure, and the trend for copying the sex culture of the Westerners are not curbed, the status of the female members of our society can not be uplifted, inspite of the opening of new avenues of progress by the State and the society.

How Have We Come and What Should We Do?

All these told above are the status of men and women from our forefathers' time to the present time. It was also stated as to how the relations of men and women changed a number of times during this period.

Science and mythology have told us various stories, how the universe and this world of ours came into existence long long ago. The birth of Adam and Eve has remained a myth. But how we are born and how our children, are born is a direct reality which is told in the very first chapter, as well in the chapter on Sex. But that does not pose much of the problems for us. If at all some problems arise, these are being solved to a great extent, by the help of modern science.

Our main problem is then the survival of the mankind, the best creation of God. But what Sir Charles Darwin referred, "Survival of the Fittest", is quite true. We shall survive only if we are fit in all respects. We, as you have already known by now, are born with the three basic elements of Love, Hate and Sex. All the three elements are indispensable for our survival. But the proportion of these vary from person to person as according to his upbringing and his environment.

As told earlier, there is a great similarity of the life pattern of plants and that of the animals. But the Love, Hate and Sex play different role in a somewhat different pattern in the plants and animals.

In the human beings, there is Love before Sex, but for the animals the Love play is not instinctual. It is generally seen that it is the male members of the animals that make all sorts of tantrums to arouse the females. As regards the element Hate, men differ widely from the animals. In human beings, it is seen that they may get aroused and then turn aggressive for only small causes or sometimes for no specific cause. This is due to his mental attitude based on his heritage and his upbringing. But for the animals, it is different. Animals get aroused and may even kill any intruder only if they are disturbed at the time of their baby feeding or when they are engaged in enjoying their own meals, or on such occasions when their self interest is encroached upon. In the human beings, the Hate element sometimes becomes so profound that we destroy things around us or kill others, or we may even commit suicide (which animals seldom do).

Though man is the best creation of God, in many respects, the animals excel in behaviour compared to human beings. Some animals and plants are said to have good memory. But what human beings can think, remember, analyse and reproduce, is not comparable to those of animals. Some birds and animals though have better sixth sense, the scientists have come to conclude that, the human 'Grey Matter' in the brain has got more furrows. Hence the human brain can be groomed for better achievements also. By grooming, this can be improved much, but to achieve this, it is pretty difficult too. Scientists opine that by cultivating, the brain faculties can be improved and harnessed to achieve difficult assignments, and sometimes, which thought impossible too.

There are innumerable examples to cite. Demosthenes had a bad speech impediment. He stammered and stuttered. He was determined to overcome this impediment of his. He had put pebbles in his month and tried to talk around. As a result he became one of the greatest orators the history has ever seen.

Panini, the great Indian Grammarian, was very bad in his studies. Once a palmist told him that certain groove on his palm is very faint and hence he is deemed to be a dunce and to remain so for the rest of his life. At that, he not only had to cut a deep groove on his palm, but also was determined to learn. Later, Panini became one of the greatest Grammarians of the time, in India.

Pitirim A. Sorokin, Director of the Research Centre in Creative Altruism at Harvard University, refers to the source of intuition as the Supra-conscious — another name for the Infinite Intelligence; — God. So, damn the atheists, grab your nearest Bible, Geeta or Quran as long as they cheer you up. But remember to read in between the lines. Faith without work is also dead. You should be sincere to yourself and sincere to your work as well. While you work sincerely, you should consider that all the jobs you do is for Him. Have faith in Him.

Over 100 years ago Elias Howe invented the sewing machine. You know how? She had faith in herself as well as in God. She sincerely thought and dreamt for a solution to stitch by means of a mechanical means. One night, she worked far into the night, fell asleep dead exausted in the bed. Her dream materialised into a reality; a sewing machine was evolved.

There are innumerable examples of how faith in yourself and faith in God combined, can make you succeed in any work. If you want to expand your knowledge, read — "Life of Emile Zola", "Life and works of Swami Vivekananda", "Life and works of Sri Aurobindo.", "Life and works of Mira Richard (known the world over as the Mother of Sri Aurobindo Asram)".

I do not mind, of your being an atheist, a non-believer of God, but mind you the persons referred to as above were all in flesh and blood. They were sincere to themselves and to God. They had faith in themselves, as well as in God. The strength and potency to achieve your goal is all in yourself. If you do not waste it, spill, spoil or destroy it, it is there to serve you to achieve your goal.

Swami Vivekananda, the 'Bireshwar or Bilay' to his mother, was an ordinary boy next door. But he had determination and faith. In the childhood, he was also an atheist like many of you. He challenged Sri Rama Krishna Paramhansa Dev decrying the concept of the Mother Kali (Indian Goddess) and her very existence. But, he had all the urge and he worked eagerly and with sincere faith and zeal to dig out the very concept of the Goddess Kali. In the day time he tried hard to solve the problem by studies and arguments and at night through his dreams and by cajoling his brain with faith. The day came when he got the answer, "God will no where to be found, but in your own soul." "Whatever you want to do sincerely, you can do." Not only he realized this, but he proved it also and preached the same, not only in India, but also in the continents far away from India. He preached the message of Love and Brotherhood throughout the globe. The gentlemen, ladies and children were to him 'brothers' and 'sisters' only.

He was able to do all these by sacrifice, meditation (through Yoga) and faith in the Almighty.

How Faith Helps us to Reach God?

A little while earlier, we have discussed how faith can cure diseases and also is able to manipulate to achieve things which we long for earnestly and sincerely.

If we pray with faith and sincerity then we surely can achieve the object or objects of our desire. Because, prayer is one of the strongest psychic forces which can activate our will power to achieve our goal. But how to cajole for the super human powers within us? It functions on a higher level than any ordinary human can control. If the superconscience is not being controlled by the human or any other spiritual energy, it must be controlled by something even greater. When you agree to this concept, may you be an atheist, hesitate not to call this spiritual energy by any name say, 'God'. This superconscious may be reached by 'Meditation', 'Concentration', 'Self Hypnosis' and complete 'Relaxation'. You must be familiar to the telephone hot line. If you can build a direct hot line with the Creator, your problems will be solved; for this, you are to turn inward.

Pray earnestly, sincerely and in seclusion. You are not to make noise or put a loud speaker, as is done by many. By doing this, your thoughts will change, the spiritual vibrations are released into the level of the Cosmic Forces. While on a prayer, as you are on the hot line for sending messages, you receive messages back in the same line too. Remember the direct "hot line works two ways."

Your sincere prayers will definitely be answered from the other side but it is seen that sometimes, you must have been praying for long, but those are not answered. You need to analyse your mental attitude. The attitude should be sincere and along with your prayers, your earthly efforts for achieving your goal should be continued sincerely also. You do not except a bolt from the blues without doing any bit of effort to achieve your goal, except those drab prayers, so as to grease the palm of the Lord.

There are innumerable examples in my life, how sincere prayers are answered. On the occasion of my son's marriage, several relatives, dropped in from far away provinces. After the marriage was over, some of our relatives wanted their valuables back from my Godrej Steel Chest. But the keys were no where to be found. All efforts to open up the almirah were futile. My wife who is a devotee of Lord Krishna, started prayers, sincerely and with full faith, to get the bunch of keys. All the time she was also making her efforts to search for the keys. Ultimately, after a search for hours, the keys were found in the dump of crushed and mutilated flowers of the previous day's functions, which were to be thrown into the river the next morning. It is not a miracle? It is not an answer from Him to my wife's prayers?

When to Pray?

Many people pray only when they feel that they are at the end of the rope, and they need immediate help. They think that they should pray in an emergency only. Prayers should be made as a regular and daily routine. It should be made a regular habit. Then the emergencies would be very few and far between. Prayers should be made in seclusion and also when your body and mind is completely relaxed. This seems to be an utopian idea. You try to relax in a yogic method and see that your body as well as mind is relaxed in no time.

In all the primary religions, it is statutory that some preparations are necessary for the starting for the meditation. Some cleanliness of the body and the mind is necessary before commencing the actual meditation. Some environmental preparation should also be there prior to the prayer.

When you are mentally prepared for the meditation, sit erect with your spine straight as far as is allowed at your age and health. Some sit on the chair, some on the floor. But there should be some sort of a thin linen under your seat to make you comfortable. In your Indian, hindu posture, you can sit cross legged, either in Padmasan or (if not possible due to age or disease) in Sukhasan pose. Plunge all your pride and prejudice at the base of the altar. All attitudes of avenge and revenge should be thrown out of your mind. Thus, when you are free and light, take a deep breadth and feel relaxed. Then utter some sentences in any language of your choice (English, Hindi, Sanskrit or any other language). These sentences should portray your mental attitude and the submission to the Creator. Thus, when you have crushed all your ego, then talk to the Creator, the way you talk to your father, elder brother or a trusted friend. Explain one of your foremost problems and ask for the guidance.

This prayer is all different from the mass prayers that is done in congregations. This prayer is your personal prayer. The time and place should be so selected that you can talk to Him in seclusion. Whatever you pray it should be private and confidential. You have booked a 'Private Hot Line Call' exclusively for yourself only. But mind you, whatever you pray for, you must have to work it up to achieve that in your private life also. If your call is earnest and your efforts are sincere, then the prayer is answered in most of the cases. The failures may be due to snags in the efforts made to achieve your goal or it may be due to any lack of sincerity in your prayer.

A few years back an Indian Bollywood Mega Star of the silver screen got severely hurt in the abdomen during the shooting of a film. He was then admitted in a renowned hospital in Bombay, where after all the trials and efforts, the experts left all hopes of his survival. At this the relatives as well as the film fans, all over the country prayed to God for his survival. The prayers were answered and he not only survived but has excelled in his future performances also.

How To Pray?

In ancient India, every known school of thought accepted Yoga as an absolute *sine-qua-non* of the ultimate achievements in life. Whether it is physiology, psychology, music, dancing, painting or even literature, Yoga had been a constant source of inspiration. Yoga represents the way of life which endows perfect health whether it is physical, mental, moral or spiritual. Basically the orthodox principles to achieve trance are through several geometrical principles, *viz:*

(a) Yama, Niama, (b) Asana,
(c) Pranayama, (d) Pratihara,
(e) Dharana and Dhyana, (f) Samadhi.

Ultimately the 'Kundalini' is awakened, wherein the narhis and nerves get activated and thus in turn help our Will Force to activate. Yoga really is a complete practical system of self culture aiming at the harmonious developments of our body, mind and the dormant psychic potencies.

To understand prayer through Yoga, we are to have some preliminary knowledge of our nervous system. Please see Fig. 5. The Central Nervous System (C.N.S.) consists of the brain, the spinal cord, and body's nerve network. The greatest number of the cell neurons are in the outer part, in the two soft hemispheres, called the Cerebrum, wherein most of the thinking and memorizing works are undertaken. Below the Cerebrum is a small brain called the Cerebellum which controls and co-ordinates various body movements.

Our main concern is the Cerebrum which controls the thinking and the memory. The Cerebrum is divided into two hemispheres, left and right which consists of the thick layers of white matter inside and layer of grey matter outside.

One end of a bundle of nerves are connected up to the *lower part of the abdomen* of which, the other end is linked to the Cerebrum. These nerves pass through the spine.

Spine, which we call as our back bone, is a flexible bony column that gives support to the body. The spine consists of small bones, called the Vertebrae, divided in 5 Sections, *viz* : Cerebral (7), Thoracic (12), Lumber (5), Sacrum (1), and Coccyx (4). The vertebrae are separated by discs of cartilages for cushioning.

At the centre of the vertebrae a complex bundle of nerves called the spinal cord is passing. And on both sides of this spinal cord, *Sympathetic nerve channels* are running throughout the length of the spine.

Prayers are possible with yoga attitude. By yoga, we activate our central nervous system. Hence, if we know our nervous system and know how to activate the same, then only we can reap the fruits of our prayers better.

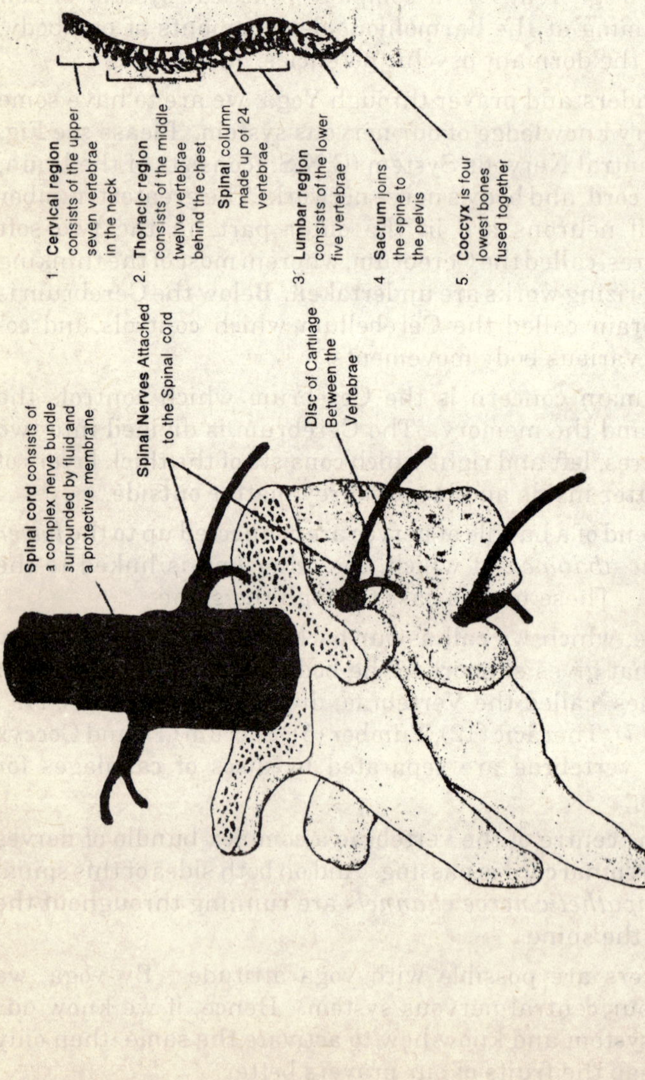

The 24 bones in the spine, called vertebrae, are separated by discs of cartilage which allow the spine to bend and cushion it frOm shocks. The lowermost bones are fused together to form the sacrum and coccyx; the sacrum attaches the spine to the pelvis.

Fig. 13 : The Vertebrae

Long before our modern medical science had come into existence, *i.e.,* before 200 B.C. approximately, the then Yogis recognised the cerebrospinal and automatic nervous system (ANS), the spinal cord. They were of the opinion that CNS consisted of 72,000 Nadis of which only 62 pairs were considered relevant. The Ida, Pingla & Susumna were all important. The famous Kalicarana said that the transmission of nerve impulses was governed by the activities of the right and the left nostrils and the breathing postures. The then Yogis were the first to recognise that nervous maladies are caused by emotions like fear, hate, anxiety etc, and these could be alleviated by pranayama, asanas and clear thinking, and that for the diseases mind is the activating factor and not the body.

In our human body, there are six nerve centres:

(1) Muladhara, at the base of the spine near the anus

(2) Swadhis Thana, at the level of the genital organs,

(3) Manipura, at the level of the naval,

(4) Anahata, at the level of the heart,

(5) Vishuddha, at the level of the throat,

(6) Ajna, at the level of the eye brows.

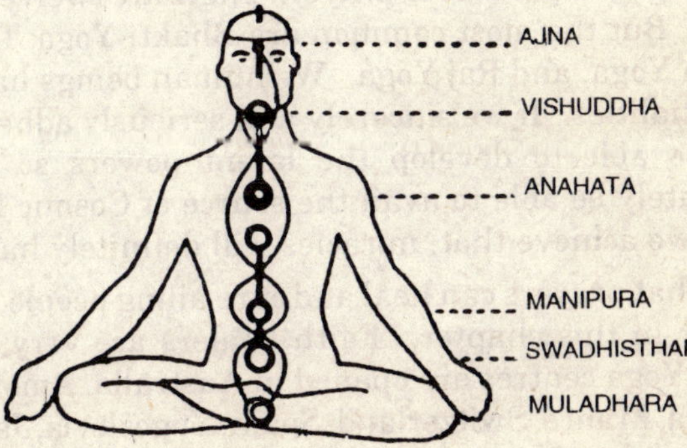

Fig. 14 : The Nerve Centres

The finer energy sources are in general, three, as given below:

(a) *Ida Narhi*: The sympathetic nerve channels that run parallel to and outside the spinal cord, on the left side of the human body is called Ida.

(b) *Pingla Narhi*: The sympathetic nerve channels that run parallel to and outside the spinal cord, on the right side of the human body is called the Pingla.

(c) *Susumna Narhi*: All these above ultimately coil round the *Sushmna Narhi* and end at the left nostril (*Ajna*).

Sushmna Narhi is in the central portion of the body.

Basically, the purpose of prayer is not to ask for material benefits. During the prayer one should inhale and exhale deeply. By doing so when you fill the body with PRANA and transmit the vibrations of peace, harmony and love to your friends and relatives, and also counteract the vibrations of enemity towards those whom you dislike. The practice of speaking out the mantras, whether it is for the christians, hindus or muslims, is to take a deep breadth so as to be able to speak out the 'Mantras'. By doing so, it induces health and calms the mind and sends out beneficial vibrations. These vibrations help to set the mind at peace and banish worry.

Yoga is a prelude to prayer. There are twelve types of Yoga in all. But the most common are Bhakti-Yoga, Dhyana-Yoga, Hatha Yoga, and Raj Yoga. We human beings have enormous potentialities. If we sincerely and seriously adhere to this, we will be able to develop the latent powers so that we will ultimately be able to avail the source of Cosmic Energy in us. Once we achieve that, miracles will definitely happen.

That prayers can heal and cure ailing people, is illustrated earlier in this chapter. Faith healers are very common and Sahaj Yoga centres are opened in Australia, America, Canada, Austria, France, Switzerland, Spain, Yugoslovia, Japan, Taiwan, Singapore and also at South-America.

Pioneer In Yoga and Prayer—Sri Aurobindo

There were many pioneers who had come and gone; but to name a few will be sufficient to inspire you for invoking for God.

Ramakrishna Parmhansa Dev

About Rama Krishna Paramhansa Dev and Swami Vivekananda, we have discussed a little while earlier. Short sketches of Sri Aurobindo and the Mother (Mira Richard) will not only inspire you, but you will be swayed by their untiring efforts and the deeds, to elevate themselves and the mankind.

Aravinda Akroyd Ghose was born to Dr. Krishna Dhan Ghose and Swaranalata Devi at 4.30 A.M. on August 15, 1872 in Calcutta. Dr. Ghose, sent his son to Manchester in England in 1879 for further studies. Arvinda was a voracious reader of European History and other works of great writers and poets. At his tender age only, he started writing poems and articles for the liberation of the human race.

After sometime he dropped his English name and changed it to Aurobindo Ghose and later he was known as Sri Aurobindo or Rishi Aurobindo. On one hand, he was the poet of patriotism, prophet of nationalism, a lover of humanity and on the other hand, he was a yogi and philosopher. At the age of 14 only, he took a pledge that one day he will work for the liberation of India. In 1921 at the age of 29, he married Mrinalini.

At the site of their family property at the Maniktola Garden, Calcutta, he, along with others, studied revolutionary literature and the 'Gita', practiced meditation and experimented to make bombs to indulge in open arm revolution in the whole of India against the foreigners. Later for a slight mistake, he was arrested with a few others in 1908 and put in the Alipore Jail at Calcutta. Sri Chittaranjan Das, the then Barrister at Calcutta, defended his case and he was thus released from the jail. He continued his Yoga and writings thereafter.

Round about his age of 32, he switched on to a vegetarian diet and started practicing 'Pranayama', with his other yoga practices. The results were remarkable. He then could concentrate better in his studies and other works. He also improved his health and his skin became smoother and fairer due to his devotion to Yoga. He used to have some aura around his head and as a result the cluster of mosquitos that were there never ventured any more to come and disturb him during his studies and meditation.

In the early part of his life, he thought that he would fight for the liberation of India with open sword. But later when he acquired knowledge, wisdom and courage, by dint of Yoga and Pranayama, he changed his mind and determined to fight for the liberation of India by his mental power only and he as well did it so.

We find some facts from the letters to his wife Mrinalini on the 30th August, 1905, which will be of interest to you. He felt (due to his meditation) that whatever virtue, talent and the wealth he possessed, belongs to God only and he had the right to spend only as much is absolutely necessary for the maintenance of his self and his family. He felt that to pray to Him in congregation is not necessary and that if one can attain the realisation that God is in the self and in the mind, then only the direct communication with God is possible. He felt that the country is not all the fields, hills and rivers, but is a living aspect like Mother. He felt that we should completely surrender to God and love this Mother and we can reach our goal.

While in the Alipore Jail in Calcutta, he used to practice Sadhana and he actually saw that his body became so light, that his whole body got lifted up against the wall during the practice of yoga.

It is told that Rishi Agastya came from the North and settled in Pondicherry. Sri Aurobindo also arrived in Pondicherry on April 4, 1910 at 4.00 P.M. Sri Aurobindo realised that there is an ascending evolution in Nature. This goes on, from stone to the plant, from plant to the animal and from animal to man. Because man is, at this moment, at the summit of the ascending evolution, once thought that men is at the apex. But, later he realised that man is not complete by himself and he thought that man is a transitional being, living in a mental consciousness but with a possibility of acquiring new consciousness what he called "Supramental Consciousness."

Sri Aurobindo's life took a turn after 1920 and thereafter, in 1926 he resumed his writings again, but for 24 years, he was virtually inaccessible. During his stay in the Alipore Jail in Calcutta, he got an *Adesh*, a message of 4 orders from the Almighty, which he did not divulge to anybody except one old associate, about the plan to place India in the forefront in the world and all the formalities thereof. He realised and was confident that the liberation of India would be possible only by Yoga and not by political means. Collective meditations began around 1922. Thereafter, it followed by discussions on a wide range of topics, *viz.*; Indian Politics, world affairs, medicines, literature, art and sadhana. He said that each religion has given us some of value to the world and that no religion as such could transform humanity.

His vital functions ceased on the 5th December, 1950 at 1.26 A.M., but the first signs of decomposition appeared on the 8th December only. His physical body remained aglow for more than 111 Hours. Recommendations were forwarded by eminent writers like Pearl S. Buck, Aldus Huxley etc. for his book "The Life Divine" in 1950, the last of Sri Aurobindo's life.

The Mother

The story of the Indian Yogi and that of the Ashram Aurovilla where his earthly body was buried in the court yard, will be incomplete if we do not speak a few words about the Mother. Mother of Pondicherry, a French woman Mira Richard Alfassa walked into Aurobindo Ashram on March 29, 1914 at 3.30 P.M. and met Sri Aurobindo there.

Mira Richard Alfassa was born in Paris on 21st February, 1878. Her father was from Turkey and mother from Egypt. She got early education at home and at about the age of fourteen. she attended a studio, to learn drawing and painting and later joined Ecole da Beaux Arts. She was a talented musician and writer also.

Between the age of 11 and 13 years, she had a series of psychic and spiritual experiences of God. At the age of 36, in 1914, she went to Pondicherry to meet Sri Aurobindo and there she recognized him as her Krishna (Indian God), who had been guiding her spiritual developments during her sadhanas abroad. In 1926, the Mother, as she was called then, was entrusted with the full material and spiritual charge of the Ashram at Pondicherry which was later branded as Auroville, after the name of Sri Aurobindo.

During her girlhood, she (the mother) was conscious of a more than human force, behind her, which often entered her body and worked there in a super normal way. This super natural force worked in several ways for her.

Once when she was seven, there was one burly boy nearly thirteen, who used to mock at all the girls. When her requests to stop that nonsense failed, she picked him up, that burly and tall boy, and threw him down with a thump. A supernatural force had come down into her and made her tremendously strong. This was recognised by herself, later in life, as the force from Mahakali (an Indian Goddess). Due to her culture of spiritual power, she acquired profuse powers, which worked miracles, several times in her life.

The Mother left her body on the 17th November, 1973 at the age of Ninety-Five.

Components of Thanatos

So far you had been undulating in love and yoga. Now, let us have a picture of a person who is a legend in the history, a monster of Thanatos. There were quite a few such who lived on the face of the globe, as well as a handful of them who are living now. Those persons were upto destroying the humanity and its vegetation, the atmosphere and the ecology in which we live in.

To deal with all such persons, it will be too much for this small book. Instead, a small sketch of the terror of Europe will be sufficient to impress upon you and to have an astringent effect on your whole body and mind.

Hitler, Adolf Hitler, who was known as *Sehiki Gruber*, his mothers' name, for the first 39 years of his life. He was born at half past six in the evening of April 20, 1889 in *Gasthof Zum Pommer*, a modest inn in the town of *Braunauam Inn* across the border from *Bavaria*. The legend goes, that he was the third son from the third marriage of his mother and a Austrian customs official. Unfortunately, as he was born an illegitimate child, he had to bear his mother's name for 39 years of his life. After getting formal education, he joined the Army in the First World War as a Private, when he was 15 only. Hitler is said to be the only single person then, who caused the death of millions of persons. It is said of him, that before he came to power, he eliminated all his rivals who were his close friends. He adopted a novel method to kill them. He used to invite them individually in a closed room and during conversations and arguments, he used to accuse them of false charges and then kill them. However, Hitler's only achievement was his book *Mein Kempf*. Though it seems strange, he was a vegetarian and a teetotaller, but used to indulge in meddling with many girls—young and old. From one of such, a French girl, was born a male child to him. But after the war was over, he lost track of the child. Again during the Second World War, when Germany occupied France, he could trace his son from the records. As he was an young man then, Hitler placed him in a high position in the Army. But, unfortunately, after the defeat of Germany, the allies came to know about this man, and then they sacked him from his post. Hitler had prepared several "dummies" who used to be sent to all the dangerous places. And Hitler himself used to go to those functions which were considered safe only. But still then, he had to die in an underground chamber along with one of his last mistresses, *Eva Braun*.

Not boring you with this man of Mortidinal nature, I shall draw the curtain of the legend of Hitler with a hilarious story, as to how he planned to share the bed with a film actress. An American actress of the silver screen has recently written a beautiful article, "My affairs with Hitler", depicting the vindictive attitude of Hitler towards the Jews. As told earlier, Hitler was a sensuous person, and as such, it is not uncommon to have any number of mistresses and to have affairs with any number of them was not uncommon with him either.

Once he was adamant to have that American actress in his bed. He thus manipulated and sneaked her into Germany via England from America. But the whole trouble started when he was about to jump into the bed, where the lady was lying. The lady was aware that Hitler stinks from the body and smells foul from his mouth. Thus the actress was fanatically trying to find out a way to avoid Hitler. During the time Hitler was undressing, suddenly she got a brain wave and threw these words to him "*Furherar*, look here, my grand father had jew blood in his vein."

At this, Hitler jumped out of the room shouting, "She is a Jewess, throw her out". Thus the actress fled and was saved.

From his short life sketch what we get is that he was an issue from a low pedigree, was sparingly educated and above all, he was addicted to illicit contacts with numerous female folks, who never married him. He wanted to kill all the Jews. As killing was in his veins, he killed millions of persons and most of them in inhuman ways.

Sex Idol Monroe

After knowing the fate of the King of Hate and Despise, you should also know the state of persons whose business was only to trade in sex and no other elements of life.

You may be able to name a dozens of them, like Christian Keeler, Madonna, Pamella Bordes (later Pamella Singh) etc. Just peep into their private lives and you will find out whether and how much happy they were!

Let us study the case of Marilyn Monroe. She was the heart throb of yester years. Her real name was *Norma Jean Baker* (or Mortenson). *Marilyn Monroe* was born in Los Angeles in the year 1926 on Ist June. She was born as an illegitimate child. Immediately after her birth, her mother's lover fled away and took away her mother also.

Seeing the condition of the child a neighbour took her home and brought her up. But that place was not a safe place either. Then there, at the age of six only, she was raped by a member of that very family. Ultimately, she was compelled to go out to an orphanage where she started earning 5 Cents only at that tender age, for washing plates and dishes. At a later stage, that very girl became a symbol of beauty and sex appeal, not only in America but throughout the world.

Due to her physical beauty and her tender and volatile features, people started casting lewd looks at her. Not only for saving herself from that situation, but also as she got many offers, she joined the film industry. Due to her physical charm she made a place in the films as an actress.

When she got some stability, Monroe married for the first time in 1942 at that tender age of 16 only. This marriage failed shortly after. She tried to be tied up in the nuptial bond again after 13 years. She might have thought that she was mature enough to keep the bond sound. But that too failed. Finally, the famous script writer Arther Miller married her. This time her luck favoured. Her film *"Bus Stop"*, released in 1955, was considered a superb *"Tragic Film"*.

She had enacted in several Films:

1. Gentlemen Prefer Blondes (1953).
2. Niagra (1953).
3. Seven Years Itch (1955).
4. Bus Stop (1955).
5. Some Like it Hot (1959).
6. The Misfits (1961).
7. All About Eve.

This was her Third Film (*All about Eve*) in which she came to the forefront and her sex appeal swept the whole of America. Her picture was published on the front pages of as many as sixteen magazines, then. And there was no end to it. After her death, that is after more than several decades, people still cannot forget her face.

Her third husband, Norman Miller, write a novel about Monroe, which was about eleven years after Marilyn's death. This book gives us many information which are not known to the common men. Every thing which has a beginning must have an end too. Hardly, Monroe crossed her blooming youth, after enjoying all the nectar of the world, and spreading her aroma to all, far and wide, she died a tragic death only at the age of thirty six in 1962. Even after so many years of her death, it is still a mystery, whether she was murdered or she committed suicide.

People say that if you live very long, then there are chances of your being unhappy sometime or other, is more. But Monroe lived only for thirty six years and rose to the pinnacle, when she was only thirty. But was she happy ever? Were people around her really happy with her? All that she had, was some sexy aura around her, which only enchanted some people but could not make them happy.

But there were so many others on the silver screen on the western globe whose enchanting acting and glamour will not be forgotten after a number of years! Similarly, on the Indian horizon also, actresses like Nargis and Madhubala, to name a few, will not be forgotten ever for all that they had. We shall ever remain grateful for those tho entertained us for years.

It is true that sex appeal of *Monroe* charmed us for several decades, but this is to be realised whether that helped her to gain happiness or could it either make people feel happy? Why this is so? Mostly because this sex appeal was not accompanied by other elements what builds up humanity. Finally, after the death of *Marilyn Monroe*, her friends and admirers were at a loss as to what should be the epitaph on her tomb. The following was considered most suited epitaph and was put up on her tomb!

"Here at last she sleeps alone."

6
CONCLUSION

After finishing the main theme of the book, we digressed on what we have learnt and what we have not.

We have seen how the Yoga exponents like *Sri Aurobindo* and *The Mother* showed us and proved that by *Sadhana*, miracles can be achieved even by the common man, if he sincerely tries to achieve these. Then we have seen the condition of the person who is devoid of love and is full of Thanatos, who inspite of his ambitions, lived a treacherous life and died unlamented. Lastly, we have also seen how the beauty queen was born, lived and died! Did you mark the note on her epitaph?

Having all that is said and done, can we analyse the basic principles on which our life is balanced?

If this chapter was told at the beginning, neither it would be palatable nor understandable. Now, that you have almost finished the book and learnt many things, you are in a position to grasp, digest and realise the truthfulness and utility of the proposition.

We have seen that when the material world disturbs our mind, we are drifted away from the golden path of truth, justice, tranquility and peace. In the language of Freud, we are drifted from Libido to Mortido.

How to check the drift from Libido to Mortido? Of course, it is a natural drift but if we can possibly check the drift or minimise it, we can save ourselves from ruining.

We need a stronger counter force to withhold the Natural Drift. If you look back to the Fig. 3, you will find that the *ID* in us, which governs our wishes should be expanded against our ego (which is governed by the reality principles).

But what is the limit of this expansion, and which also is the method that will help us to execute this expansion?

Let us first understand the domain of *ID* and its functions? *ID* is that division of mind (psyche) that is the seat of Libido. This Libido arouses the animalistic and chaotic impulses that demand only gratification.

But the Ego, which, if we can develop properly and steer meticulously to win over *ID*, the Ego will be able to distinguish between the Self and the Environment. There is a big 'but' in it. If this Ego is not able to develop properly, due to unsuitable environmental situations, as well as self assertiveness, the *ID* takes over. Then the Libido is free to play its flute and to mould us in any way our body wants.

It is to be kept in mind that the Libido is both life instinct and the death instinct, that is the Eros and the Thanatos. If this Libido is not tackled properly, and the death instinct Thanatos takes a lead then the story takes a bad turn.

What, then is there to help us, to save our soul from this catastrophy? Libido broadly include all kinds of love and pleasure, but finally it encompasses both the life and death instincts. This was conceived first by Dr. Freud. But Carl Jung, (1875-1962) a Swiss Psycho-analyst and founder of Analytical Psychology, who also became a member of Freuds' Circle, later disagreed with what Freud said, over the nature of Libido.

Libido plays a great part in shaping our character. To throttle the activities of Libido, there is no other way than to take help of the "Great Cosmic Force".

It seems thunderous! But in reality the process is simple. The only thing that is necessary, is to "Dedicate us to Ourselves". We are to swim out into the 'Void', mentally and try to have "Total Emancipation". In a way, we are to "Annihilate to the Eternity!" For this process, it is not at all necessary to change our material and social life.

This needs some practice to reach the "Absolute Void." If you sit down in solitude and try to be physically and mentally silent (this is Absolute Silence!) and thinking of nothing for a few moments, when, of course, those moments may be terribly frightening, you will feel as if you are crumbling down into an abyss, and "Absolute Void". This is a transformation from the "Outer Consciousness" into the "Inner Consciousness".

At times, you must have seen that whenever you fall short of ideas or energy, to cope up with the present situation of future commitments you need some extra energy. Certain energy that you already have, needs some recharging. This recharging cannot be done by the intake of some extra rich food or medicines.

If these do not agree with the constitution of your body, then those may have adverse effects on you also. You need some permanent and suitable solution.

What you need is the "Universal Vital Force", which you can have if you have a contact with "Nature". There are numerous other methods to commune and revitalize your energy to work more and with courage. But this one that is to strike a contract with Nature is very spontaneous. If you enter into contemplation and call down the forces to have higher and better life, this will rejuvenate your energies. As a matter of fact, as according to the Second Law of Thermodynamics, "The Total Energy in the Universe is Constant. It can neither be created nor destroyed". Similarly your "Internal Vital Energy" is also constant. But how to supplement your Internal Vital Energy when you want to boost it?

Some people think that 40 is the age when you start collecting money for the future, so that you can be calm and composed at the old age. Money earning is one, but you are to enrich yourself in many other ways mentally, so that enhanced knowledge and wisdom can make you richer and happier. This is one way to get more from outside your mind.

Similarly, there is another way of getting more physical and mental energy to withstand the external jolts that we get from time to time and consume our own "Internal Vital Force".

An example will elucidate, how unnecessarily we spend and consume our own Internal Vital Energy. It is seen that most of the time we speak or argue unnecessarily. Teachers and preachers only have utility talk But in general, we consume and waste our Internal Vital Energy in futile talks. You should be soft spoken and less spoken, if you want to safeguard your Internal Vital Energy from waste. When a person is "Angry", he physically and verbally wastes much of this Internal Vital Energy.

One example was for fighting with people. Another example is for fighting with the 'Nature'. If you cannot love 'Nature', Nature will hate you, and reject you also. Do not fight with the shadow and waste your Internal Vital Energy. Many people hate almost all the seasons of the year. No weather is becoming of them, whether it is summer, rainy season or the winter."

Whether it is human being, or animals, we are constitutionally so built that our body can adjust automatically unless we disturb the system. Some change is automatic and the rest is achieved by our personal efforts. We have not to grudge about it. Only we should be mentally prepared for the occasion and for the situation. The Africans do not complain about the atmospheric heat, nor the Eskimos for their cold. It is only we, who are brought up in ideal and protected atmosphere and conditions, do grudge and grin.

Let us take a different view of the situation. Trust in 'Nature' and 'Nature' will cater to your needs. Nature is not tailored to your needs. You are to fill in the crevices to suit your comfort. As regards the seasonal changes, call in the Universal Vital Force or rather invoke for the same, and you will find a miracle. The earnest prayer will be listened to and the Universal Vital force will be there on your side to help and assist you. Once you are able to invoke the Universal Vital Force, it will surely recharge your Internal Vital Energy. Then the job is done. We will be able to stand all the calamities and all the adverse climates.

In our long journey through life, we are definitely to meet emergencies and exigencies and at those times, we fall short of our Internal Vital Force. At those times, if we can invoke the Universal Vital Force, then we can get relief. But if we are not accustomed to that sort or prayer all along, then in emergency, we may feel difficulty in invoking the Universal Vital Force. Why not then make a routine to keep some time reserved for prayer everyday? Truely speaking, if we give true respect to the Nature and the Cosmic Force, we will have a natural bent of mind to bow down to the Creator and feel the Cosmic Force always on our side. This will give us Tranquility, Peace and Pleasure.

BIBLIOGRAPHY

S. NO.	*NAME*	*AUTHOR*	*YEAR*
01.	Conquest Of Happiness	Bertrand Russel	1955
02.	Yoga aasns Simplified	Sri Yogendra	1959
03.	Phychology Made Simple	A.P. Sperling	1967
04.	Family Health Guide	Readers' Digest	1972
05.	Yoga Illustrated Dictionary	Harvey Day	1972
06.	Sri Aurobindo	Navajata	1972
07.	How Your Psychic Powers Can Make You Rich?	D.ST. Clair	1975
08.	What Islam Is?	M.M. Roman	1979
09.	Mayers' Midwifery	Betty R. Sweet	1982
10.	Dictionary Of Psychology	Eric Berne	1987
11.	Sri Aurobindo	Peter Heehs	1989
12.	Living Within	A.S. Dalal	1990
13.	The Great Adventure	Sri Aurobindo Ashram	1991
14.	Time (Magazine)	—	1991
15.	Sunday Mail (Magazine)	—	1992
16	The Telegraph (Magazine)	—	1993
17.	Few Clippings From Newspapers	—	1990